Milwaukee Walks - Again

Historic Neighborhoods
County Parks
The Lakefront
Outdoor Sculpture
Two Breweries
And a Few Restaurants

by Cari Taylor-Carlson

Serendipity Ink   Milwaukee, Wisconsin

Serendipity Ink
P. O. Box 17163
Milwaukee, WI 53217

Library of Congress Catalog Card Number 97-66507

First Printing 1997

Illustrations: Lynne Bergschultz
Editing: Gina Taucher
Production: Cheryl Gorton
Printed by: McNaughton & Gunn, Inc.

ISBN 0-9629452-4-2

For my friends who walk with me,
sharing my enthusiasm for
Milwaukee's neighborhoods,
the lakefront and the small restaurants
we discover along the way.

Other books by Cari Taylor-Carlson

Milwaukee Walks - Twenty Choice Walks in a Classy City

The Upscale Outdoor Cookbook - Simple Recipes for Campers, Backpackers, and Short-Order Cooks

Milwaukee Eats - An Insider's Guide to Saloons, Cafes, Diners, Dives and Neighborhood Restaurants

The Food Lover's Guide to Milwaukee - An Insider's Guide to Ethnic Bakeries, Grocery Stores, Meat Markets, Specialty Food Shops and Cafes

To order write:
    Serendipity Ink
    P. O. Box 17163
    Milwaukee, Wisconsin 53217

Acknowledgments

Thanks to my friends in the Milwaukee Walking and Eating Society who patiently followed me on walks into most of these neighborhoods. A special thank you to Don Nichols who plotted the "Greendale Maze Challenge" and then miraculously took me through the village on this challenging but fascinating route. Thanks to Chris O'Brien, Nancie Baker and Pat Morris who led me to resources I used in my research. Thanks to Nina Witsell who directed me to Seminary Woods when I thought I would never ever find this elusive place.

Finally a standing ovation for my capable and diligent team Gina, Cheryl and Lynne who can take a rough manuscript and turn it into a book in two short months!

Historical street information is quoted from *Milwaukee Streets: The Stories Behind Their Names,* by Carl Baehr, Cream City Press, 1995.

Introduction

*I*n 1991 I wrote *Milwaukee Walks - Twenty Choice Walks in a Classy City*. Six years later I offer a new set of twenty walks, this time with an added historical focus. In my first walking guide, I described neighborhood strolls. This book is different. For six years, since *Milwaukee Walks* was published, I've scouted neighborhoods looking for perfect routes for these new walks.

When I first mentioned this project to friends their typical comment was, "Oh that's nice. You must be updating the first twenty walks." Wrong! Why should I repeat myself? Milwaukee offers an impressive number of historic neighborhoods surrounded by parks and parkways. Plus, we have the lakefront. After all, Milwaukee is "A Great City on a Great Lake." Lake Michigan touches neighborhoods, both city and suburban, from Bayside to South Milwaukee. I could design twenty more really interesting walks with every one touching the lake at some point along the route, but that would be another book. Meanwhile, in this book, six walks include the lake, the beach, the bluffs and even an island.

From the impressive Milwaukee County Park System, I chose eighteen parks and parkways to include in *Milwaukee Walks - Again*. From Doctor's Park in Fox Point to Grant Park in South Milwaukee to Grobschmidt Park in Franklin, I found dozens of walking routes that weave between parks, parkways and neighborhoods.

Settled by groups who emigrated from Germany, Poland, Ireland, Italy and Great Britain, to mention a few, Milwaukee's neighborhoods reflect a European diversity. There are Polish flats on Lincoln Avenue, Italianate Revival homes on Yankee Hill and German-inspired country homes on Layton and McKinley Boulevards. Many neighborhoods have kept their distinctive personalities, because Milwaukee has resisted bringing in the wrecking ball and calling it progress. We're aware of the importance of restoring historic homes, commercial buildings and neighborhoods.

There are a couple of different ways to take these walks. One could think of "Along the Lakefront," a five mile walk, as a chance for some hard and fast exercise. Or, one could choose to saunter around this loop, spending a leisurely Saturday morning contemplating the beauty of our downtown lakefront. Then follow the walk with a cheese omelet and American fries at the Pavillion Restaurant near the Mark di Suvero sculpture. Either way, it's a good walk.

In 1991 I wrote in the introduction to *Milwaukee Walks*, "I'm proud to live in a Midwestern city where limiting a walking book to just twenty walks turned into a challenge."

That was six years ago, and it's still true! Now that *Milwaukee Walks - Again* is finished, I'm ready to start the sequel. I could call it "Twenty More Milwaukee Walks - Again!" I can restrain neither my exuberance nor my need to share this city with other walkers.

The best way to see Milwaukee is on foot. I hope you have as much fun with these walks as I did while I planned, walked, researched and wrote this book.

C T-C
1997

Freeways and Major Streets

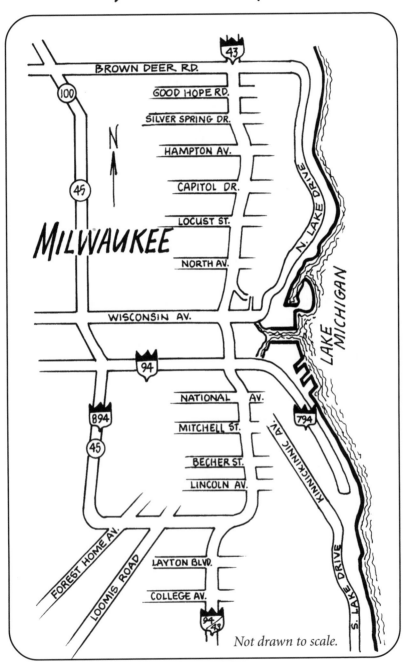

Not drawn to scale.

Table of Contents

A long the Lakefront

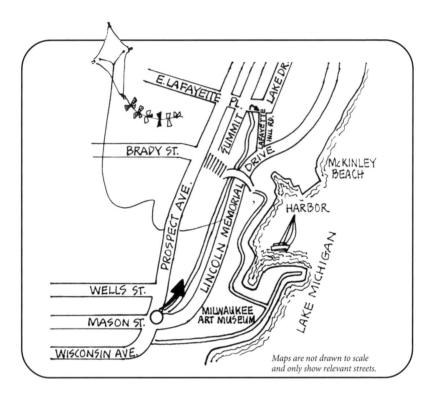

Maps are not drawn to scale
and only show relevant streets.

Distance - 5 miles

HIGHLIGHTS
Bike Trail, sculpture, the lakefront, Veterans Park and Juneau Park

WHERE TO PARK
On Prospect Avenue just north of Wells Street, where it's not metered

HOW TO GET THERE
Drive east on Wisconsin Avenue to the end of the Avenue and curve left onto Prospect Avenue to Wells Street.

THE ROUTE
Start at the intersection of Mason, Prospect, Lincoln Memorial and the Bike Trail. Walk north on the Bike Trail. At an intersection just before

the tunnel that would take you to North Avenue, bend right and walk uphill to the corner of East LaFayette Place and North Summit Avenue. Cross LaFayette Hill Road and walk down McKinley Hill. Cross at the light and turn south on Lincoln Memorial Drive. Just before the Brady Street bridge turn east and head across the grass toward the harbor. Follow the harbor past the pavilion and out to Lake Michigan. At the lake, detour left and walk to the end of the walkway. Turn back and follow the walkway uphill toward the Milwaukee Art Museum. Keep walking until you intersect Prospect Avenue and return to start.

J've walked past this Benjamin Hawkins sculpture dozens of times without seeing it. The sculpture, a flagpole, was presented to Milwaukee in 1932 by the Milwaukee Chapter of the Service Star Legion. Organized in 1918, this group sells the well-known red poppy to support World War veterans. To honor the men and women who died in foreign wars, the Service Star Legion has commissioned hundreds of war memorial statues all over the United States.

Soon after this flagpole was placed in Milwaukee in 1932, it became a magnet for out-of-town visitors. However, this is not the flagpole's original location. Until 1979 it was located at the intersection of Wells, Plankinton and 2nd Streets. Ironically, on September 24, 1968, the flagpole was a rallying point for Vietnam War protesters who undoubtedly were unaware of the significance of the statue.

From the intersection follow the Bike Trail, and after about 100 feet you'll see a rather large boulder. I couldn't help wondering if it was placed here to add character to the park or if it was an "erratic," a leftover hunk of rock from the glacier that scoured this land 10,000 years ago.

As you come into the woods, notice the ubiquitous white flowers on 8-12 inch stems. These unwelcome plants, known as garlic mustard, have turned into a major problem for Milwaukee County parks. Many plants in the mustard family are lovely, with four petals forming a cross, four sepals and usually six stamens. However, this member of the mustard family does not belong here, and in time, garlic mustard will blanket the woods, choking out every other plant.

There's also too much litter. Perhaps the county should consider organizing groups to "adopt" sections of the Bike Trail to help keep it clean.

Along this section of the trail, I like to visualize how it must have looked one hundred years ago. The present day park to the east is built on landfill; Lincoln Memorial Drive would have been under water. Perhaps today's bike trail was a bluff behind a sandy beach where families came to picnic on Sunday afternoons.

As you leave the trail and exit at the top on McKinley Hill, take a minute to enjoy the grand view of the harbor. This is a good walk on a hot day, for the breeze off the lake almost guarantees the "cooler by the lake" effect.

At the bottom of McKinley Hill, cross Lincoln Memorial Drive carefully at the light. Rush hour drivers sometimes confuse the speed limit here with the 70 mile-per-hour limit on the freeway. Head across the grass toward the harbor, past a perfectly formed oval maple tree. Follow alongside the harbor to the parking lot near the kite shop and the picnic pavilion. Here you'll see boats with names like "Contentment," "Sea Dog," "Dry Martini" and "Misprint." Walk straight ahead to Lake Michigan and turn left at the "T" for a short but scenic detour to the end of the walkway. A stroll here can have a dangerous edge on a summer evening between 5:00 and 8:00, when the after-work joggers, bikers and skaters come out for serious exercise. Look out! You'll recognize them; they're the ones making time, heads down, dripping sweat as they move to some interior rhythm.

However, this remains one of my favorite walks. The views are great and many friendly people walking children and/or dogs will return a cheerful greeting. A long time ago this walk was lake and beach. I once heard a teacher explain this landfill phenomenon to her class. She got their attention when she said, "You are sitting on a large garbage dump."

At the Bike Trail "Lake Loop" sign, walk straight ahead to Lincoln Memorial Drive. You might want to take a short detour to examine the sculpture on the grounds of the Milwaukee Art Museum. I'll name the four pieces and let you decide which is which. For detailed information about any of the sculpture in this book, refer to *Outdoor Sculpture in Milwaukee* by Diane Buck and Virginia Palmer.

The four sculptures are "Delicate Balance" (1968) by Tal Streeter, "Calipers" (1967) by Forrest Myers, "Monumental Holistic III" (1978) by Betty Gold and "Argo" (1974) by Alexander Liberman. Here's a hint to help you match sculpture to name: Gold is interested in geometric forms and Liberman in the relationships between positive and negative space.

LaFayette Place

It would be almost un-American not to have a street named for the Frenchman, Marquis de LaFayette. After the Revolutionary War, where LaFayette gained his fame, American cities began a new practice in street naming. Instead of just calling their thoroughfares for trees or destinations or functions, developers and city leaders started the now popular tradition of naming streets for people, particularly those whom they admired. LaFayette was much admired, as demonstrated by the nearly one thousand streets named for him around the country.

Milwaukee got its LaFayette when Second Street was changed to LaFayette Place in 1875.

Walk up the hill on Lincoln Memorial to view the sculpture of Abraham Lincoln. Here you will learn that Milwaukee was incorporated on January 31, 1846. This statue was a civic effort that began in 1916 when Mayor Daniel Hoan organized a fund drive. He collected $23,000 in corporate gifts as well as nickels and dimes donated by children. An impressive 61 artists competed for the honor of creating Lincoln's likeness. Italian sculptor Gaetano Cecere took 18 months to complete the 3000 pound sculpture, dedicated in 1934. Because "simplicity is what I strove for in this work," he left off the famous beard to more accurately show character in Lincoln's face.

To the left, at the end of Wisconsin Avenue, notice the Mark di Suvero sculpture, "The Calling," also known as "Sunburst." A friend of mine calls it "that red thing at the end of Wisconsin Avenue." It's been controversial for a number of reasons, including the steel beam construction, the simple design and the fact that an anonymous citizen donated $100,000-$200,000 for the work. Is it art? I leave it to the reader.

Another landmark at the end of Wisconsin Avenue is the large clock on the Pavillion Restaurant. It came from the Northwestern Railroad Station, sadly torn down in the 1960s. The restaurant is worth a stop if only for a cup of coffee and the view. The food is good, the variety impressive and the portions generous. They're open 24 hours a day, 7 days a week and in 1996 a cheese omelet made with three eggs, American fries and toast cost a mere $3.95. If it's a nice day, the patio will be a fine place to enjoy a meal and to congratulate yourself on the completion of a five mile walk.

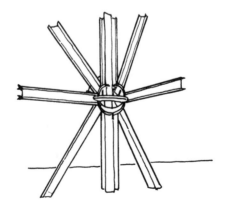

The Beer Barons' Promenade

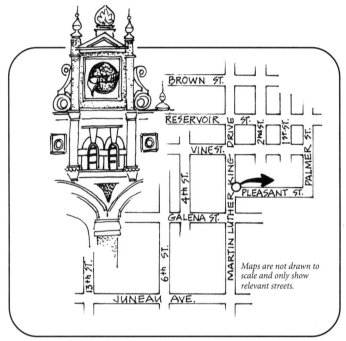

Distance - 3.5 miles

HIGHLIGHTS
Brewer's Hill, Schlitz and Pabst Brewery complexes

WHERE TO PARK
At the corner of North Martin Luther King Drive and West Galena Street

HOW TO GET THERE
Interstate 43 north to North Avenue. East on North Avenue to Martin Luther King Drive (3rd Street)then south to Galena Street.

THE ROUTE
East on Pleasant Street, north on Palmer Street, west on Reservoir

Avenue, south on 1st Street. West on Vine Street, north on 2nd Street, west on Brown Street, south on Martin Luther King Drive, west on Vine, south on 4th Street. At Galena cross the 6th Street bridge, then south on 6th to Juneau Avenue, west on Juneau to Pabst, return on Juneau to Martin Luther King Drive and start.

*T*his route twists and turns because I want to give you a tour of Brewer's Hill plus a view of two of Milwaukee's historic breweries, Schlitz and Pabst.

The walk begins at the Schlitz Brewing Company complex. Or as we've all heard, "Schlitz! The beer that made Milwaukee famous!" More than any other product, beer built the reputation and created the social life of 19th century Milwaukee. The Schlitz Brewing Company was founded by August Krug in 1849. When Krug died in 1856, the firm's German bookkeeper Joseph Schlitz gained control of the company. After Schlitz lost his life on a steamship journey to Germany in 1875, the Uihlein family took control of the business until 1982, when Stroh Brewing of Detroit bought the company.

Some of the buildings were subsequently destroyed but a few remain to give us a flavor of the 19th century architecture. Look for the Stock House at the corner of Galena Street and North Martin Luther King Drive, with its bulbous copper dome and ornamental tiered gable reflecting exuberant German Baroque architecture.

As you walk inside the complex from Pleasant Street, you'll see The Brown Bottle, a German-type rathskeller built in the 1930s to entertain Schlitz guests. In Germany, a rathskeller is an eating and drinking establishment located in the basement of the town hall. The Brown Bottle dining room features ornamental carved woodwork and hand-forged light fixtures made by Milwaukee's Cyril Colnik. The food is good too!

The Bottling House at 1560 North 2nd Street was built of cream city brick. It's a good example of a German stepped gable. The Stable Building at the corner of North 2nd and West

Pleasant Streets features lifelike figures of horse heads and shows again the German love of bold sculptural detail. The stables housed the big draft horses that pulled the beer wagons.

On Pleasant Street, Sax Arts and Crafts, located in the lower level of the former F. Mayer Boot and Shoe Company, is a good place to shop for art supplies.

Turn north on Palmer Street, walk up a slight hill and enter Brewer's Hill. This is the oldest intact neighborhood in Milwaukee, bounded by North Avenue, Walnut Street, Holton Avenue and Martin Luther King Drive. This land was originally a bluff overlooking the Milwaukee River. On top of the bluff a forested plain stretched to the north. By 1837 streets ran in a north-south orientation and Green Bay Plank Road became 3rd Street (now Martin Luther King Drive). This was a fashionable shopping street.

Brewer's Hill was a self-contained German community with buildings and homes reflecting the heritage and the diversity seen today. You'll see Federal style, Italianate, Greek Revival and Victorian homes on these few blocks. Most of the homes were built by German immigrants between 1850 and 1910. By the turn of the century, other Europeans were beginning to filter in to Brewer's Hill and as the years passed, they were replaced by blue-collar workers.

The area began to decline in the 1960s but the 1970s brought "urban pioneers" who purchased homes and began to restore them. These shabby, boarded-up mansions had been in need of major work, but they now show signs of their former glory.

Today the neighborhood houses a population as eclectic as the architectural styles found here. This is a close-knit neighborhood with a strong Neighborhood Association. Residents have the will to improve their neighborhood and to keep their streets safe.

If you walk around Brewer's Hill in summertime, take a look at the gardens as well as the homes. Walk north on Palmer and detour one block both east and west on Vine Street before continuing to Reservoir. There are many interesting homes in various stages of restoration on Vine. Be sure to notice 215 with its million-dollar view from the back deck. Other homes of note are located at 134, 114 and 102 Vine.

Back on Palmer notice the Greek Revival home at 1818 and the Italianate cream city brick mansion with its extensive perennial gardens at 1823. Now walk west on Reservoir, south on 1st, west on Vine, north on 2nd and west on Brown to Martin Luther King Drive. Before heading south on King, detour ½ block north to 2034, the Northern Chocolate Company, built in 1885.

Many of the buildings along the next few blocks still have their original facades dating from 1835-1900. At that time this street was a commercial hub serving Brewer's Hill and many homes to the south and east.

Turn west on Vine Street and at 325 you'll pass an inconspicuous sign "Carreau du Nord"or "Tiles of the North." The owner of this studio, open by appointment only, makes wrought iron furniture and hand-made tiles.

Turn south on 4th Street past Golda Meir School and walk west to cross the 6th Street bridge. Here you have another million-dollar view of downtown Milwaukee. Head south on 6th and west on Juneau to the Pabst Brewing Complex.

Although Pabst closed their doors, the company remains a giant in the history of the American brewing industry. Pabst was founded in 1844 as the Best Brewing Company by Jacob Best, a German immigrant. In 1862 Captain Frederick Pabst married Best's granddaughter and became president of the brewery. By 1900 their German-recipe beer was famous and Pabst was the world's largest brewery.

The Brewing Complex is a Locally Designated Milwaukee Historic District. It includes the Gift Shop and Reception Building at 901 West Juneau; the Office Building Complex at 915-17; the Bottling House at 1100 North 10th Street; the Pabst Saloon and Restaurant, a former church at 1037 West Juneau;

and the Pabst Brewing Company Saloon at 1338 West Juneau.

This is the end of the brewery tour. Follow Juneau back to Martin Luther King Drive and walk north back to start. Take your time because there's much more to see in this neighborhood.

Juneau Avenue

Solomon Juneau, (1793-1856), came to Milwaukee from Canada about 1818 as an agent for John Jacob Astor's American Fur Company. In 1820 Juneau married Josette Vieau, the daughter of a Menominee Indian woman and a Frenchman who traded in Milwaukee. In the mid-1830s Juneau formed a partnership with Morgan L. Martin in developing Milwaukee Village. Juneau, considered the founder of the city, was its first postmaster and its first mayor. In later years he moved to Theresa, Wisconsin, which he named for his mother.

There have been serveral streets named for Juneau; this one, which he called Division Street in 1835, was renamed Juneau Avenue in 1885. Juneau Park and Juneau County are also his namesakes.

A Circuitous Route

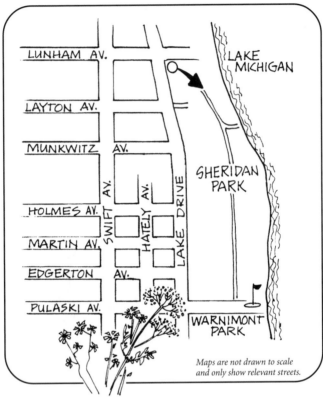

Maps are not drawn to scale and only show relevant streets.

Distance - 4 miles

HIGHLIGHTS
   Sheridan Park, Lake Michigan, a Cudahy neighborhood

WHERE TO PARK
   At the corner of Lunham Avenue and South Lake Drive

HOW TO GET THERE
   Interstate 94 south to Layton Avenue. East on Layton to South Lake Drive and north on Lake to Lunham.

THE ROUTE
   Cross Lake Drive and walk south on the Bike Trail. At the first

junction turn east and detour to Lake Michigan. Return to the Bike Trail and turn west at a sign for Warnimont Golf Course. Cross Lake Drive and continue west on Pulaski Avenue. Then right on Hately Avenue, left on East Edgerton Avenue, right on South Swift Avenue, right on East Martin Avenue. Left on Hately, left on East Holmes Avenue, right on Swift, right on East Munkwitz Avenue, left on Lake Drive. Detour into the park at Layton, return to Lake Drive, back to start.

You'll start next to the Welcome to Cudahy sign. Cudahy was Milwaukee's second industrial village thanks to Patrick Cudahy, who located his meat packing factory in this area adjacent to the Chicago and Northwestern railroad route. Cudahy became a village in 1895 and a city in 1906, when it had a population of 2556. After another major factory employer, the Ladish company, moved in, Cudahy became known as a blue-collar city, with German, Irish and Eastern European residents. Although most of these people lived in Cudahy close to Lake Michigan, the commercial life of the community took place on Mitchell Street. Today Cudahy remains a working-class town without a major commercial center.

Instead, Cudahy has neighborhoods where dozens of well-tended middle class homes are in various stages of renovation. On the eastern edge of the city, Sheridan Park adds a green spot of beauty to this South Side neighborhood.

Please walk carefully on the Bike Trail. If you're in the middle of the trail when a bike comes around a corner, you're vulnerable. After all, you're in their right-of-way.

If you come here in late August or September the field just off Lake Drive will be a painterly mix of white daisy fleabane, blue bergamot, yellow evening primrose, purple chicory, blue milkweed and cream-colored Queen Anne's lace with splashes of goldenrod. Since you're close to Lake Michigan there's always a breeze and a splendid view of the Milwaukee skyline.

Walk past the peaceful lagoon and take a minute to watch

children fishing, sailing small boats and catching frogs. At a junction where a trail goes east, take it and switch back down an old road to the lake. I'll almost guarantee privacy. The only person I saw on my last visit was a tan, fit middle-aged man doing push-ups on a jetty, three jetties down the beach. I sat quietly and enjoyed watching his hard work.

The rectangular concrete jetties were placed on this remote beach in Sheridan Park in the 1930s to build up the beach by catching sand as it washed ashore.

It's quiet here. There's nothing to disturb the sounds of waves breaking on shore, a gentle breeze and the buzz of an occasional plane overhead. Maybe you'll see a flock of long-legged, long-billed birds walking so fast at the water's edge that their legs are a blur. These nervous-appearing birds are sandpipers. They rush back and forth following the receding waves in hopes of harvesting whatever tasty morsels the lake washed ashore. It's entertaining to watch them as they stay less than an inch ahead of each wave.

Walk back up the hill to the Bike Trail and when you come to the sign for the Golf Course, turn right. Walk due west across Lake Drive past the Fountain Blue Restaurant and continue west on East Pulaski Avenue. From here follow the route on pages 20-21 to find your way through this quintessential Cudahy neighborhood. Enjoy the stroll and watch for the homes in various stages of renovation. Because many residents are making creative changes, the neighborhood is interesting to visit.

Walk north on South Lake Drive back to Layton Avenue and take a short detour on Cudahy War Memorial Boulevard to view the Patrick Cudahy Memorial and the Cudahy War Memorial. The War Memorial is engraved with the names of soldiers lost in World War I, World War II, the Korean War and the Vietnam War. A time capsule, dedicated in May 1992, will be opened in 2015.

The Patrick Cudahy Memorial was commissioned in 1965 by Cudahy's eldest son Michael. The sculpture by Felix de

Weldon captures Cudahy in the role of self-assured business-man. I'll guess Patrick, who died in 1919, would have liked this confident model of himself.

Return to South Lake Drive and walk back to start.

A good place for a meal is the Fountain Blue Restaurant at the corner of Pulaski and Lake. The eclectic menu includes several Polish specialties served in a dining room with a central fountain. This restaurant also has a beautiful classic Milwau-kee-style bar with old wood and leaded glass.

Cudahy Avenue

Patrick Cudahy Jr., who founded the city of Cudahy, was born a few months before the family left Ireland in 1849 to escape the potato famine. His career in the packing business began at the age of 13 when he worked at a Milwaukee meatpacking firm for $3 a week as an unskilled laborer. He became a foreman, then a superintendent. By the time he was in his early thirties he earned $50,000 a year as plant manager for Plankinton and Armour, when the average annual income was less than $500.

When he was 39 he took over the Plankinton company, renamed it Cudahy Brothers (his brother John provided significant capital for the company), and a few years later moved the operation to its current Cudahy location. The company name was changed again in 1957 to Patrick Cudahy, Inc. When Patrick died at the age of seventy in 1919, he was reported to "have paid the heaviest income tax" in Milwaukee and was termed one of its wealthiest citizens.

In 1892 Patrick, perhaps with help from John, named the streets of his company town after business associates. Most were in the meat trade. Some were in the raising of cattle or hogs, others in the slaughtering or packing of them. A few were brokers and others were retail butchers. Most were from the Midwest and many had their roots in Ireland. In later years, as the city of Milwaukee expanded southward, its new streets took on the already established Cudahy street names.

Circumnavigate a Downtown Island

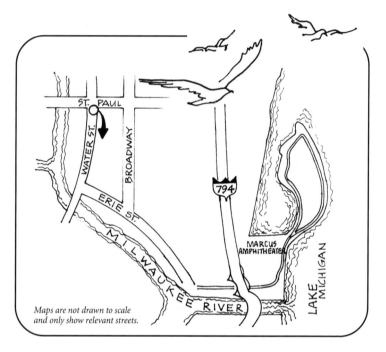

Maps are not drawn to scale and only show relevant streets.

Distance - 3 miles

HIGHLIGHTS
  Third Ward and Summerfest / Harbor Island

WHERE TO PARK
  North Water Street, south of St. Paul Avenue

HOW TO GET THERE
  Take Interstate 794 east, exit Plankinton Avenue, east on St. Paul Avenue to Water Street.

THE ROUTE
  South on Water to Erie Street, southeast on Erie across the large parking lot toward Lake Michigan, under the Hoan Bridge. Behind

Marcus Amphitheater, enter Harbor Island, walk around the Island, return across the parking lot to Erie to Broadway, north on Broadway to St. Paul to Water and back to start.

*T*his walk is a jewel since it's unknown to most Milwaukeeans. Only the fishermen know about it; they come to fish off the boulders on the east side of the island.

To add extra pizzazz to this walk, I have a suggestion for intrepid walkers. I have yet to do this myself, but I've always wanted to take this walk by the light of a full moon.

The route starts on Water Street in the Third Ward where parking is easy and where one can find dozens of interesting shops. Right on Water Street where you left the car, Great Lakes Futon and Water Street Antique Market both offer good browsing.

Follow Water south to Erie Street and pause at the historical marker for the Lady Elgin. On September 8, 1860, the Lady Elgin sank while returning from Chicago, when she collided with an unlit, overloaded lumber schooner and 300 passengers perished. The Irish Union Guards had chartered the ship for a fund-raiser, so most of the passengers were from the Third Ward. This tragedy decimated Milwaukee's Third Ward Irish community.

Along Erie Street you'll see the back side of the Third Ward as you follow the Milwaukee River out to the harbor. You'll have a great view of the Hoan Bridge, a $25,000,000 arched suspension bridge, winner of the 1975 Long Span Bridge Award from the American Institute of Steel Construction.

As you cross the railroad tracks, note the rectangular Bridge Tender's building that's been remodeled as a private residence. When you come to the barricade and the "Road closed to thru traffic" sign, don't worry, you're on foot. Head across the parking lot toward the back of the Marcus Amphitheater, cross under the Hoan Bridge and follow the lake shore to Harbor Island or as it's sometimes called, Summerfest Island.

Circumnavigate a Downtown Island **25**

The breakwater light at the entrance to the harbor, constructed in 1926, is the principal navigational light for the Milwaukee Harbor. It rises five stories above the water. Until 1963 it was operated by rotating four man crews who worked for 21 days, then spent seven days on land. Now automated, it's controlled by a station on South Lincoln Memorial Drive.

Harbor Island was dedicated for "public use and enjoyment" by Milwaukee Mayor John Norquist on October 9, 1991. The best part of this walk is the view from the island where you can see downtown, Bay View, the industrial valley, the Prospect Avenue skyline, Lake Michigan and the Milwaukee River.

It's always cool here. This is a great place to sit on a rock on a hot summer day, feeling the cool breeze while surveying the spectacular view. If you leave your watch at home as I tend to do, the clock at Allis Chalmers will tell you the time and if you care, the temperature.

Water Street

Before 1836, Water Street was a trail along the Milwaukee River. In June of 1836 it became the first street in the city. Sylvester Pettibone, behind a plow pulled by eight oxen, graded the new street to the cheers of early Milwaukeeans. The group then began a Milwaukee tradition of celebrating significant (and sometimes not so significant) events with food or drink. They consumed 30 baskets of champagne to mark the event. The street was platted by Solomon Juneau and Morgan L. Martin in 1835.

To complete the walk, retrace the route back to Erie Street until you come to Broadway. Erie and Broadway Streets don't technically meet but instead are connected by a walkway. Broadway has a gentrified appearance, new since I published *Milwaukee Walks* in 1991. Enjoy the street, the shops, the benches and the opportunity to engage in some entertaining people-watching. Along the way you might want to visit the Broadway Theater Center where the Skylight Theater has a new home. It's gorgeous.

There are good places to stop for a meal around here. I recommend La Boulangerie, Wild Thyme Cafe and Bon Marche. If it's breakfast time, enjoy a good cup of strong coffee and a tomato-mozzarella omelet at "La Bou." If it's lunch time, try a sandwich at Wild Thyme. For dinner I suggest everything on the menu at Bon Marche, but make a reservation if it's a weekend.

Turn west on St. Paul and return to start. The only problem one might encounter on this walk will be parking during Summerfest. On the other hand, that might be a good time to stay clear of this area. Unless of course you enjoy traffic jams and the congestion all those Illinois people cause when they come to Wisconsin's festivals.

A little off the route on Chicago Street is a personal favorite, the Italian Community Center Restaurant. Their food is fantastic, prices reasonable, portions generous and the staff is consistently friendly and welcoming.

East Side Neighborhood Trek

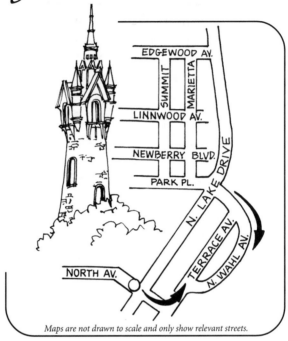

Maps are not drawn to scale and only show relevant streets.

Distance - 4 miles

HIGHLIGHTS
The North Point area on the East Side

WHERE TO PARK
At the corner of North Lake Drive and East North Avenue

HOW TO GET THERE
Interstate 43 north to North Avenue. East on North Avenue to North Lake Drive.

THE ROUTE
East on North Avenue to Terrace Avenue. Northeast on Terrace, north one block on Wahl Avenue to North Lake Drive. West on Edgewood to Summit Avenue, south on Summit to Linnwood Avenue, east on

Linnwood to Marietta Avenue, south on Marietta to Newberry Avenue. West on Newberry to Summit, south on Summit to Park Place. East on Park to Wahl Avenue, south on Wahl to North Avenue and back to start.

*T*his walk can be taken in two ways. You might choose to simply walk the four mile lopsided square without paying much attention to the homes, or you could choose to read the text of this book and take a more leisurely stroll. Along the way, you'll learn something about a section of Milwaukee that's filled with historically and architecturally interesting homes.

To learn more than the bits of information provided in this book, consult *The Heritage Guidebook* by H. Russell Zimmermann. Begin on page 83 in the North Point chapter.

Many of the homes in this neighborhood reflect the heritage of the well-to-do Germans who built them. Wanting their homes to resemble those of the prosperous merchant and industrial classes in Germany, wealthy Milwaukee Germans kept informed of architectural trends in their homeland. The homes they built, many of them in the North Point Historic District, were often showy and considered avant-garde. Many of them were built around the turn of the century. As you walk this loop, notice the gables, turrets, steep roof lines, helmet-shaped domed towers and sculptural terra cotta ornaments. The era of building in the German Renaissance style was brief; by World War I a modernist movement surpassed the influence of European design.

You'll walk in an area known as North Point. This designation comes from location, as it's the farthest north shore of Milwaukee Bay. Milwaukee Bay is the southernmost of three bays, Milwaukee, Whitefish and Donges. In 1854, two far-sighted residents, Jefferson Glidden and John Lockwood subdivided one hundred acres and established this neighborhood. Then, as today, it was a prestigious location, bounded on the south by East North Avenue, on the west by the Milwaukee River, and on the north by Edgewood Avenue. Lake Park, one of Milwaukee's most beautiful parks, is on its eastern edge.

Start this neighborhood trek at the east end of North Avenue at the Water Tower. When this elaborate Victorian Gothic tower was built in 1873, it stood next to a cow pasture. The tower was built to cover an iron pipe, four feet in diameter, that was used to absorb the uneven water pressure from the old steam pumping engines.

You're standing across the street from St. Mary's Hospital, Milwaukee's oldest and Wisconsin's first public hospital. The original hospital was built in 1856 in that pasture next to the Water Tower. It was soon torn down and replaced by the hospital we see today.

On Terrace Avenue take a look at 2420. This Frank Lloyd Wright home with its tile roof and wide overhang is typical of Wright's "prairie" home designs. Next, notice the German Renaissance-style home at 2611. Known for its stained glass windows and its gargoyles, it is one of Milwaukee's most flamboyant German-style residences. It was built in 1900 for Gustav Trostel, whose father Albert had opened the first tannery in Milwaukee in 1858.

Walk to the end of Terrace and follow Wahl to Lake Drive. You'll pass a par three golf course and part of Lake Park. Continue walking north on Lake Drive to Edgewood. Don't miss the unusual row of copper beech trees just before you come to 3252 Lake Drive.

Turn west on Edgewood and south on Summit and enjoy a quiet street lined with well-tended upper-middle class homes. Many of these homes have been renovated since the 1960s. The fix-up at 3243 Summit is a good example.

When you come to Linnwood, turn east, then south on Marietta and follow Marietta to Newberry. Two homes worth seeing on Marietta are 2937, a spectacular Victorian "painted lady" and 2835, another Victorian, this one painted white. We called it the "whipped cream" house.

Turn west on Newberry, walk back to Summit and follow it to Park Place. Then walk east on Park Place, cross Lake Drive to Wahl and follow Wahl Avenue south to North Avenue.

There are many homes on Wahl worth a second look. At 2623, the Dr. James A. Bach home was built in 1903. This Victorian style is called Austrian Renaissance. The exterior ornamentation is extravagant and since this home was included in the popular book, *Daughters of Painted Ladies*, it has become a local celebrity. At 2601 you'll see a different look, an English Cotswold-style home, built in 1922.

In the 2500 block are two more German Renaissance-style homes at 2569 and 2543. The first, the Kern mansion, was built in 1899. It was similar to villas built in the suburbs of German cities such as Berlin. Notice the ornamental iron by Cyril Colnik, a master craftsman and well-known Milwaukee ironworker.

The home at 2543, built in 1901, has a wealth of exterior sculptural detail including terra cotta panels, human faces and winged dragons. The love of sculptural detail makes this house unusual; it showcases the German love of fine craftsmanship and carved decorations. A different look at 2409 is the Robert Nunnemacher residence built in 1906. It was designed to resemble an English 17th century manor home.

The gardens at the corner of Bradford and Wahl are also worth a stop. I've admired these formal gardens on both sides of Bradford for many years. I marvel at the energy-intensive care they require, as well as the love of the land and impressive gardening knowledge they demonstrate.

Follow Wahl to North to start. If you're in the mood for a Mexican meal, Jalisco's on North Avenue is a fine place for a cold beer and an oversized chicken burrito. You can eat like a king and walk away with change from a ten dollar bill.

An Eclectic Suburban Hike

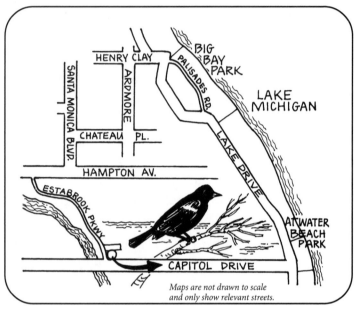

Maps are not drawn to scale and only show relevant streets.

Distance - 6 miles

HIGHLIGHTS

Atwater Park, Big Bay Park, Estabrook Park, charming Lake Drive homes and Whitefish Bay

WHERE TO PARK

Lot #8 in Estabrook Park

HOW TO GET THERE

Interstate 43 north to Capitol Drive. East on Capitol to Estabrook Park. Turn north into the park and drive a short distance to lot #8.

THE ROUTE

Return to Capitol Drive and walk east on Capitol to Atwater Beach Park. Then follow Lake Drive north to Big Bay Park. Where Lake turns west go straight on North Palisades Road. East on Henry

Clay Street, south on Ardmore Avenue, west on Chateau Place, south on Santa Monica Boulevard, west on Hampton, south on Estabrook Parkway back to start.

A long walk through Shorewood and Whitefish Bay may leave your legs tired, but the walk is well worth the effort thanks to the diverse attractions along the route. From traffic on Capitol to solitude alongside the Milwaukee River, this walk won't disappoint intrepid walkers willing to trek six miles.

The Sandwich Emporium at the intersection of Capitol and Oakland Avenue is a fine place to begin or end this walk. The Emporium moved into this location in March 1997, when Daily's suddenly vacated the premises. By reputation, they make fine sandwiches. The owners had a small shop on Capitol Drive just east of Oakland for many years.

At 2214 East Capitol is Saint Robert's Catholic Church, a point of historical interest. The cornerstone for this Romanesque church was laid August 12, 1936. The variegated red brick walls are decorated with insets of different colored marble. Notice the oak doors enhanced by brass studs.

Cross the street at Prospect Avenue to see a collection of contemporary paintings, glass and pottery at the Fine Art Framing and Gallery. As you continue walking east, traffic will gradually subside until you cross Downer Avenue and residential quiet replaces urban bustle. From here to Lake Drive the homes are attractive and the walk relaxing.

At Atwater Park take a minute to enjoy the birds and Lake Michigan, or walk down the new steps to the beach. The park dates to 1931 and, as was the case with many Milwaukee County parks, was a federal relief project during the Depression. Workers built a beach house (no longer there), installed drain tiles to prevent erosion of the fragile bluff and built a cement block path to the beach. The fountain, by prominent Milwaukee sculptor Paul Yank, was commissioned in 1969 and donated to the village of Shorewood by Mr. and Mrs. Oscar H.

Keehn. In 1994 Atwater Park was given a facelift. Now, many benches provide a place for private thoughts while you enjoy the lake view.

The next two miles take you past some of the North Shore's finest homes. This is a popular walking route because there's so much to see. The sidewalk on the east side of Lake Drive offers a continuous walk, because all the connecting streets end at Lake Drive. You'll see graceful old homes, well-kept gardens, grand old trees, walkers, joggers, dogs on leashes and through the trees, Lake Michigan.

When Lake Drive curves to the west in Whitefish Bay, continue straight ahead to North Palisades Road. Here you'll find Buckley Park, a village park, adjacent to Big Bay Park, a Milwaukee County park. If you follow the blacktop path to the old pier and look north along the shoreline, you can clearly see the outline of Whitefish Bay and you'll understand why it's called a bay.

Return to Palisades by way of the old stone steps, but watch out for the red-winged blackbird that nests close to the top of the stairs. He's known to dive-bomb innocent pedestrians. I know he's a male, because he's black with red wings, while the female is soft brown with a striped vest.

At the north end of Palisades notice the landscaped yard behind the black fence. This garden sits on top of landfill dumped in the 1980s to save the bluff and Big Bay Park. Someone did a masterful job of reclaiming this land and turning it into a spectacular garden.

Lake Drive
Lake Drive, which runs along Lake Michigan for most of its length, was formerly known as Fourth Avenue until an ordinance renamed it in 1875.

Cross Lake Drive and follow Henry Clay Street to Ardmore Avenue. Turn south on Ardmore and walk past the former Whitefish Bay Armory, home of a division of the Wisconsin National Guard. At the corner of Henry Clay and Ardmore, you're standing on the site of a former resort developed by Captain Frederick Pabst in 1889. Pabst built a 250 foot long pavilion here to rival the Schlitz Palm Gardens as a place to drink beer. The dining rooms featured fresh fish caught daily in Whitefish Bay. By 1914, the resort closed, the buildings were torn down and this prize real estate along the lake was subdivided for homes.

One of the well-known homes at 5270 (a short detour north on Lake Drive) is the Italian Renaissance mansion built in 1918 for Herman Uihlein. It's built of buff Bedford limestone taken from a single level in a single quarry and carved on-site to avoid potential damage.

Return to Ardmore and walk south to Chateau Place. Follow Chateau to Santa Monica Boulevard, Hampton Avenue and Estabrook Parkway, then back to start at lot #8.

When you come to picnic area #5, you have two choices. You can take the "high road," the paved bike trail that dips and bends as it follows the parkway, or you can take the "low road," an often muddy trail that goes alongside the Milwaukee River for 1½ miles through the park.

Pick up the latter at lot #5, where stone steps in front of the lannon stone building lead to the Milwaukee River. This trail has a sense of Milwaukee pre-settlement, as it was once an Indian trail. It's isolated and not a good place for a solo walk.

If you decide to follow the trail, be aware that certain unavoidable problems may arise. If you encounter mud, bugs or uneven terrain, several sets of stairs will take you back to high ground. Beware of the occasional mountain biker who may come screaming around a corner on this trail. I had an encounter with a biker when I walked here on a May day and I know if my reflexes had not propelled my body instantly off the trail, a messy collision would have resulted.

However, walking this trail feels like adventure. After you come to the cables for the radio station across the river, watch for a group of massive willow trees. Here's where the path leaves the river. Climb the winter sledding hill and you'll come out across the parkway from lot #8. Watch for a large stone near the stone building. According to legend, Indians placed corn and other grains in the hollow indentation on this stone and pounded them into coarse flour to use in making bread. The stone looks as if it could be part of an oversized mortar and pestle.

Before you leave the park, detour north to the small white Benjamin Church Home, a fine example of Greek revival-style architecture. The house was built in 1844 and moved to this site from North 4th Street in 1938. Its Doric columns and fine proportions make it a Milwaukee treasure. If you take this walk in summertime, you may find the home open to the public. The tour is especially interesting because the home contains much of the original furniture.

Return to start. Across Capitol, Riverbrook Restaurant was built on the site of the former well-loved Pig and Whistle. The food is cheap and pretty good and there's plenty of it.

A Fox Point Stroll

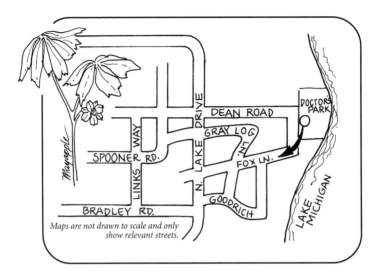

Maps are not drawn to scale and only show relevant streets.

Distance - 3.5 miles

HIGHLIGHTS
Doctor's Park, Lake Michigan, lovely homes in a beautiful wooded setting, textbook examples of landscape artistry

WHERE TO PARK
In the parking lot at Doctor's Park

HOW TO GET THERE
Interstate 43 north to Good Hope Road exit. East on Good Hope to North Lake Drive. North on Lake Drive to Dean Road. East on Dean Road to Doctor's Park.

THE ROUTE
South and west on Fox Lane to Goodrich Lane. South and west on Goodrich to Grey Log Lane. Follow Grey Log around the curves across Lake Drive to Spooner Road. A short west on Spooner then south on North Links Way to Bradley Road. East on Bradley to Lake Drive. North on Lake Drive to Fox Lane and east and north on Fox Lane back to start

The path leading through the woods to the beach at the north end of Doctor's Park seemed magical to me in 1972. A newcomer to Milwaukee from Peoria, Illinois, it meant I could live near Lake Michigan and life would resemble the summer vacations I spent by Lake Michigan in my youth.

Doctor's Park is still a special place, especially on a misty day when most people stay close to home. The path to the beach, actually more like a road, takes one into a ravine through a maple-basswood forest, where a springtime visit means a chance to see some of southeastern Wisconsin's early wildflowers. If you're one of those people who grouse about spring, claiming the season lasts 15 minutes in a good year, you should visit Doctor's Park on a sunny May day.

You'll see wild geranium with its five pink petals. According to folklore, this flower symbolizes constancy and availability, and if one is so bold as to send it to a lover, the message will be "I desire to please you."

You'll see trout lily, a plant with narrow spotted leaves that look like the outside flesh of a brook trout. The inconspicuous yellow or white lily is known as the "sacred flower of motherhood." It offers an incentive to mothers, for the leaves allegedly make a tea that will cure hiccups. But don't even think about picking a flower or a leaf, because it takes a trout lily seedling seven years to produce a bloom.

You'll see mayapple, one of the first plants to push and shove its way through last summer's leaf litter. Some people call it umbrella plant after its widespread leaves. Only the plants with double stems will produce flowers; the single stemmed mayapples are sterile. The mayapple has a white flower hidden under its broad leaves but don't try to transplant it, for according to folklore, if a woman moves a mayapple, she will become pregnant.

You'll see trillium, another member of the lily family. All the trillium's flower parts are in threes, giving it its name, a Greek word for three.

Follow the path to the beach and take a few minutes to enjoy one of Milwaukee's greatest treasures, Lake Michigan. Since Doctor's Park is one of the coolest places in the county, bring a picnic on a hot July day and stay awhile. There's plenty of open space to toss a Frisbee.

Tired of the park? Head out through the parking lot and walk south on Fox Lane. If you wonder why it's called Doctor's Park, watch for the eight stone pillars and a plaque that reads, "The gift of Doctor Joseph Schneider. Eminent physician, true humanitarian and ardent lover of nature. Dedicated by him to my fellow citizens for recreation purposes, its natural beauty to be preserved and bird life to be fostered. July 11, 1928." Dr. Schneider had a country home on this site and donated his land to the City of Milwaukee. In 1937 the land was turned over to the county. Unfortunately, Dr. Schneider's country home was torn down. He would have enjoyed seeing children romping in the park and hearing the cheerful sounds of their laughter.

On the adjoining land, the fenced-in cemetery was the site of the Fox Point School built in 1852. The cemetery was officially dedicated in 1868 but its earliest grave is dated 1854.

The rest of this walk is just a walk and an opportunity to enjoy viewing some of Milwaukee's finest homes. Set into forests adjacent to Lake Michigan, these homes, beautifully landscaped, present an excellent lesson in Horticulture 101. Annuals, perennials, carefully placed shrubs and trees, hedges and spectacular lawns all advertise the hard work and creativity of residents and landscape contractors.

These roads don't go anywhere. There are no sidewalks but there's no need for them so it's safe to walk in the street. After crossing Lake Drive and making your way to Links Way, Bradley Road and back to Lake Drive, follow the path on the west side of the drive back to Fox Lane. Walk east on Fox Lane and return to start.

The North Shore Bistro would be a good place for a meal after your Fox Point Stroll. The Bistro is located nearby in the

NorthPoint Shopping Center at the corner of Port Washington and Brown Deer Roads. After such a healthful walk, roast eggplant on focaccia would taste just right.

Calumet Road

Calumet is the French word to describe the peace pipe used by North American Indians. It was considered almost sacred by Indians and would normally guarantee safe conduct to those who offered it. When the French explorer LaSalle offered a calumet to an armed group of Potowatomi Indians near Milwaukee in 1679, not only was his peace overture accepted, but the Potowatomis gave a feast in his honor and provided food for his journey.

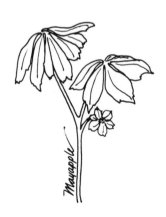

The Greendale Maze Challenge

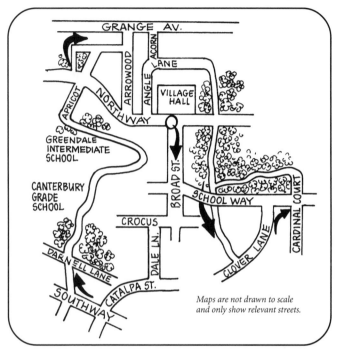

Maps are not drawn to scale
and only show relevant streets.

Distance - 3.5 miles

HIGHLIGHTS

A 1936 post-Depression, government-planned community known as
a "Greenbelt Town"

WHERE TO PARK

In the municipal parking lot off Northway and Broad

HOW TO GET THERE

Interstate 94 south to 894. West on 894 to Loomis Road (Highway
36) and southwest on Loomis to Grange Road. A short west on
Grange to Northway and left on Northway to the Village Hall.

THE ROUTE

Follow the map! ! ! and the directions in the text of the walk.

$\mathcal{T}$hanks to the Greendale Historical Society, I have background information about this walk. In 1936 the U.S. Department of Agriculture developed three communities called "Greenbelt Towns." One of these towns was Greendale. The Department had three main objectives in this Depression program: to demonstrate suburban planning that combined both city and country living, to give middle income families housing at reasonable rent and to give jobs to thousands of unemployed workers. These jobs were meant to provide long term social and economic benefits to the community.

To this end, the government purchased 3400 acres of farmland southwest of Milwaukee and laid out a community with a "greenbelt," parks and farms surrounding the future suburb. In this plan, residential streets would surround a centrally located business district. In 1938 when the village opened, residents could meet all their shopping needs in this business center. According to plan, they could walk to the stores without having to cross a major street.

The government owned the homes until 1949 when occupants were given the opportunity to purchase them. By 1952 all the transfers were complete and the government was out of Greendale.

In 1997, parks and open spaces continue to be integral to Greendale and these green areas in the middle of the village make it unique among Milwaukee suburbs. As you walk this walk, you'll visit these "greenbelts."

Start at Northway and Broad at the Village Hall. It looks just like it did when it was built in 1938. As you cross Northway and walk south on Broad you're looking at the block that was the original Village Shopping Center. Here you could feast on a 35 cent fish fry washed down with a nickel beer at the tavern. Along this street you could also pick up the mail, buy new shoes, get a haircut, deposit your paycheck in the bank and go to the movies.

At Schoolway take a look at the flagpole and its sculptural base. Built in 1939 by the WPA artist Alonzo Hauser, the figures represent working people.

Keep walking south and enter Dale Lane. Ignore the sign that says, "Do not enter." Some of Greendale's older homes are located on Dale Lane. Their tiny garages tell of an earlier time when cars were small and most families had just one to keep in the garage.

Most of these homes have tile or slate shingle roofs and are built of "cincrete," a kind of cinder block. Instead of expensive basements, each unit has a first floor utility room for the furnace and laundry facilities. Many homes still have the original coal chute. The first level usually had asphalt tile flooring on a concrete slab while the second level had oak or maple floors. Most living rooms had ponderosa pine-beamed ceilings and used the wood sub-floor of the second story as the ceiling.

Turn right on Catalpa, right on Southway and right again at the first sidewalk. Cross Darnell Lane and walk into the woods. You've entered a turn-of-the-century woods containing maple, black cherry, ironwood, basswood and other trees associated with a hardwood mix. As you walk north, bear right past Greendale Intermediate School, then left through the basketball courts and back into the woods.

There's a surprising lack of litter in this urban forest. Someone cares. As you walk this section, you'll see woods to the left and homes to the right. Pass Azalea and Arbutus and huff up a small incline. Turn right at the home with the impressive backyard deck and enviable hot tub. Now you're on Apricot, a street that resembles a lane one might find in an English garden village. The massive "village blacksmith" spreading oak tree on the southwest corner of the Apricot / Northway intersection adds a 19th century ambiance.

Cross Northway, turn left, then right into Pioneer Park, then right again at the walkway. At the north end of Apricot Court notice the twin two-bedroom homes with the "bachelor apartment" in the middle. The bachelor's quarters are tiny, located above the garage where allegedly only a single male would choose to live.

Leave the walkway at Arrowwood Street, turn left, then right on West Grange for one block, then right on Acorn Court. Stop at

5503. There are two things to know about this site. First, when the government opened this original model home in 1937, the public coming to see it caused major traffic jams on Grange. Second, this home is located close to a site where an Indian burial ground was discovered ninety years ago. This suggests that Greendale was once the site of an Indian village.

Turn left on Angle Lane and when you come to the end, keep walking straight across the wooden bridge, then turn right. This is the part of Greendale where the sidewalks are adjacent to the back yards instead of going between the private homes. This route gives walkers a more personal view of the back yards. Noting the absence of laundry lines, I asked around and learned from a resident that Greendale has an ordinance that forbids hanging out one's laundry. Keep following this backyard route across Northway all the way south to Clover Lane.

Turn left on Clover, right on Schoolway, left on Cardinal Court and bend left onto another "greenbelt" walkway. A wonderful backyard playground along here is every kid's dream.

After you come off the walkway, cross the wooden bridge again and turn right on Schoolway. It will take you back to Broad and back to start.

A good place for a burger, onion rings and great frozen custard is the inimitable Kopp's at the corner of 76th Street and Layton Avenue. On my last visit, the daily special, "chocolate chip cookie dough" custard was just reward for navigating the "Greendale Maze."

Getting to Kopp's isn't easy. Here's a hint: since you can't get there from 76th, plan to start early to move into the left lane in order to make the turn onto Layton. Then you can enter Kopp's from Layton. It's quite confusing and traffic is heavy but it's well worth the effort when you sink your teeth into that delicious custard.

A Historical Walk

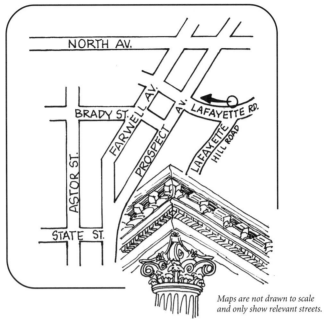

Maps are not drawn to scale and only show relevant streets.

Distance - 2.9 miles

HIGHLIGHTS
   Prospect Avenue, known as King's Row or the Gold Coast, Yankee Hill
   and Brady Street

WHERE TO PARK
   At the corner of LaFayette Place and LaFayette Hill Road

HOW TO GET THERE
   Interstate 43 north to North Avenue, east on North to Farwell, south
   on Farwell to LaFayette Place, east on LaFayette Place to LaFayette
   Hill Road (top of McKinley Hill).

THE ROUTE
   West on LaFayette Place, then southwest on Prospect Avenue to State
   Street, one block west on State to Astor Street, north on Astor to
   Brady Street, east on Brady to Prospect and back to start.

There's so much to see on this walk, why not make a day of it? Start with breakfast at the Brady Street Pharmacy. I promise you won't be disappointed by their Belgium waffle a la mode. Try it with butter pecan ice cream if it's available, then pour warm maple syrup over all and enjoy.

The walk officially starts at the corner of LaFayette Hill Road and LaFayette Place. You're standing at the top of McKinley Hill looking at the harbor, McKinley tennis courts and the Hoan Bridge, with a wide-angle view of Milwaukee's skyline. Enjoy the view from two well-placed benches or stretch your legs and sit on the grass in the shade of the honey locust tree.

Walk west on LaFayette Place and turn southwest on Prospect Avenue. After you pass "apartment row" for the next several blocks, you'll come to 1962, the Shorecrest Hotel. This is one of Milwaukee's first high-rise buildings, built in two stages in 1924 and 1928. The Prospect Avenue section was a 1928, $400,000 addition to the eight-story building that fronted on Summit Avenue. Nearby at 1930, the Park Lane Apartments demonstrate art deco styling in a high-rise apartment, decorated with variegated buff brick trimmed in glazed terra cotta.

Don't miss Lakeshore Montessori School in the next block. It's the salmon-colored building with green and red trim and a colorful sunflower painted at the second floor level. The building was once the home of the Kane family who owned most of this neighborhood. Across the street is Saint John's Home and their recently annexed addition, the former Cudworth Legion Post. The former Post sits on the site of a Civil War Camp, Camp Reno, where 7000 men prepared for war.

Across the street, the Charles Allis Art Museum is housed in a Tudor mansion built by Charles Allis, first president of Allis Chalmers Manufacturing Company. Two blocks farther down this "Gold Coast," the former E.D. Adler residence is one of the late Victorian mansions still standing on the East Side. Its eclectic design shows elements of both Queen Anne and Romanesque styling, as seen in the asymmetrical gable and tower. At 1584, the Wisconsin Conservatory of Music was once the residence of Charles L. McIntosh who owned a controlling interest in J.I. Case Company in Racine. Notice the sheet metal cornices and balustrade, the four Corinthian columns and the impressive portico. This splendid home housed a 25 by 50 foot music room and dance hall in French 18th century style. Next, the Fred T. Goll residence at 1550, most recently the offices of Ogden Realty, is a fine example of an Elizabethan manor home. Notice the corbels with carved heads. Across the street at 1537, the Elizabeth Black residence, done in English Renaissance, is an impressive red building. Notice the cornices and cut limestone quoins. Today it's divided into apartments.

Down the avenue at 1451, a classical building known as Renaissance Place is available for rent for private gatherings. At one time it was the First Church of Christ, Scientist. The grand entrance with four Doric columns would offer a fine entrance to an elegant party.

At 1363, there's a spectacular Victorian mansion built by grain broker Gilbert E. Collins. Inhabited by his daughter Ella and her husband Edward Ewell, the home has an unusually complex roof line composed of many segments. It is currently the home of Park Travel.

At the corner of Prospect and Knapp, a bronze statue of Robert Burns was a gift to Milwaukee in 1909. Donor James Anderson Bryden wanted the city to have a statue of his favorite poet. This triangular intersection is now a tiny park called Burns Square.

Prospect Avenue

James H. Rogers named this street in 1847. The street, on the bluffs, offered a pleasing view, or prospect, of Lake Michigan. Rogers, born in New York in 1794, put a $1,200 value on his land along Prospect Avenue from Juneau Avenue to Brady Street, and west to Humboldt Avenue. He died in 1863.

At the corner of Prospect and Juneau Avenues, walk toward the lake turning in at a white iron gate to Frederick and Company, Inc. Investments. This gate may or may not be open but if it is, you will enter a prime piece of real estate on the Lower East Side. If the gate is closed, you can still peek through the bars.

You'll see three more Gold Coast homes on Prospect before turning west on State Street. The first at 1229, built by Frances Hinton, is a three story townhouse that allegedly blocked Judge Jason Downer's view of the lake from his mansion at 1201 Prospect. Downer retaliated by blocking Hinton's view with another three story townhouse at 1223 Prospect.

Next you'll come to Prospect Avenue's oldest home at 1216, built by Stephen A. Harrison in 1866. Pierced bargeboard gives it a distinguished look. The third historic mansion is the home of Jason Downer at 1201. This Victorian Gothic residence began as a church in 1869. When the church fell on hard times in 1874, the judge bought the foundation and built a home.

In the late 1800s, out-of-town guests were often given a tour of Prospect Avenue and its grand homes. Many changes have taken place on this street, originally a Sauk Indian trail. Today the buildings remind us of the wealthy settlers who followed the Indians and owned this spectacular land on high bluffs overlooking Lake Michigan.

Turn west on State Street to see the lovely Dr. Henry Harrison Button residence, now David Barnett's Gallery. You have come onto the high ground east of the Milwaukee River known as Yankee Hill. Some of Milwaukee's earliest and finest homes were built on this land. The area was named after the first settlers, Yankees from New England and New York State. Notice the Eastern influence in the street names, Astor, Marshall, Franklin, Jackson, Van Buren and Jefferson.

Walk north on Astor Street to 1037, the former James K. Ilsley residence, patterned after a French chateau. With steeply pitched roof lines and dormers with finials, it's a gem and still a private home. The James S. Brown home at 1122 North Astor was built on the highest point between the river and the lake. Brown was Milwaukee's 11th mayor, subsequently elected to Congress. His home today is the elegant Zita, a clothing store with valet parking.

In 1895 John Barth built a home at 1331 North Astor. This was a large step up for Mr. Barth, a child of German immigrant parents. He built his German Renaissance Revival-style home in the middle of a neighborhood settled by well-to-do Yankees. Notice the flat facade and the dramatic gables of this house.

Wander down any of the side streets in Yankee Hill to see more of these mansions built by Yankees. The vintage homes you'll see make these detours east and west from Astor well worth your time.

At Brady Street turn east and enjoy a gentrifying neighborhood that's never dull. Hungry? Stop for an evening meal at Au Bon Appetit, one of Milwaukee's top 25 restaurants and an ideal place to rest and to enjoy a genuine Lebanese meal. Look for Chef Rihab Aris in a red hat that matches her red lipstick. Not only will she greet you with her beautiful smile, she'll serve you some of the best food in Milwaukee.

Along Brady Street you'll find many shops, cafes and miscellaneous places to explore. I recommend Sciortino's Italian Bakery and Glorioso's Italian Market. Follow Brady across Farwell back to Prospect Avenue. Turn north on Prospect and return to start.

A Leisurely Loop

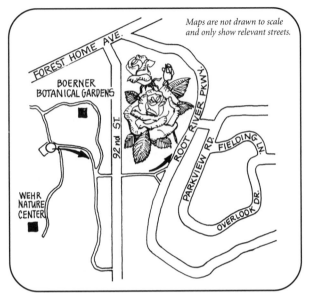

Maps are not drawn to scale and only show relevant streets.

Distance - 5 miles
plus detour to the Botanical Gardens

HIGHLIGHTS
  Whitnall Park, Boerner Botanical Gardens, Root River Parkway and
  a Greendale neighborhood

WHERE TO PARK
  Picnic areas # 5 and #7 in Whitnall Park

HOW TO GET THERE
  Interstate 94 south to I 894. Take 894 to the Forest Home exit. Take
  Forest Home Avenue to South 92nd Street. Turn south, go to the
  entrance to Whitnall Park and follow signs to Wehr Nature Center.
  Beyond the turn-off for the center continue to parking for picnic areas
  #5 and #7.

THE ROUTE
  Follow the park road back out of the park and turn left at the Root

River Parkway. Then turn right at the first road. Turn right again on Parkview Road and follow Parkview (at some point it becomes Overlook) to Fielding Lane. Turn left on Fielding, right on Parkview, left at the unmarked intersection and left again at the Root River Parkway. Turn right at the fork and return to start. Detour to the Botanical Gardens by turning right at the sign for the gardens then walk up hill to the gardens.

*M*y favorite time to walk in Whitnall Park and visit the Botanical Gardens will always be the month of May. There can't be a more splendid sight than hundreds of crabapple trees in bloom on a sunny warm day, when all shades of red and pink blossoms are silhouetted against a deep blue springtime sky. Add a gentle breeze, bird songs, a whiff of freshly mowed grass, a few puffy cumulous clouds floating above, and this is paradise found.

The walk starts in Milwaukee County's largest park, acquired in the 1930s and named after Charles B. Whitnall, a County Park Commissioner. Known as "the father of the parkway system," Whitnall's foresight was astounding. He showed his vision when he said, "Parks in congested districts are good. But do not stop there. Remember that out beyond the city's boundaries lie broad acres where trees yet naturally flourish, where there are natural water courses, where there is cheap land and limitless space. . . Go there and make your best parks because in time the city will spread out. Let it spread around these parks." Prophetic words indeed.

Whitnall Park, a collection of old pastureland and a few woodlots, wasn't much to look at before the Park Commission acquired it. Today it's a gem with ponds, gardens, woodlands, a golf course, grassy hillsides, Wehr Nature Center and the crown jewel of the park, the Boerner Botanical Gardens.

As you follow the road out of the park toward the Root River Parkway you'll come to a sign that says, "Geese Crossing." Geese do cross the road here between the two ponds, moving slowly in a stately manner as if they think they're something special. I'd rather see them here than on a golf course where they often take up residence, showing no respect for the sport of golf and crossing the fairway at the most inopportune moments.

Take a minute to sit on the stone bridge constructed by the Civilian Conservation Corps, a fine place to rest on a warm sunny afternoon.

Walk west to the Root River Parkway, turn left on the parkway and left again where the road forks. The parkway is an example of a "green belt," again showing foresight on the part of the early park commissioners. Their plan was to beautify county streams with landscaping and to connect them to big parks with drives. While giving us green belts, they also prevent small streams from becoming dumping grounds. As one travels the extensive parkway system around Milwaukee, it's clear those early objectives were met.

Follow the parkway to an unmarked road and turn east, then south on Parkview Road. The next two miles are a leisurely loop through an upscale Greendale neighborhood. There are no sidewalks but since there's also no traffic, this is a safe place to walk in the street.

This neighborhood contains more textbook examples of creative landscaping. There's marvelous diversity here with abundant deciduous and coniferous trees planted in carefully landscaped yards. After you cross Fairmont Lane you'll notice that the homes are newer and the trees appear younger.

Walking a circle in this neighborhood is like walking in a park. Each yard seamlessly adjoins its neighbor creating an unbroken mass of immaculate lawns and gardens. One could think of this walk as a stroll through the Greendale "House and Garden Theme Park." Each house differs stylistically from the others and the overall effect suggests an ideal suburb where Ozzie and Harriet might reside if they lived in the 1990s. The homes in this neighborhood have a strong continuity in their architectural features, as do others in this book, such as Cold

Spring Park where the homes reflect the German influence, Lincoln Avenue with a line of Polish duplexes or even Yankee Hill with blocks of European-inspired mansions. One wonders what new homes will look like in 2047.

As you walk the loop, don't be confused when Parkview turns into Overlook Drive. Keep walking to Fielding Lane, turn west, then north on Parkview, west at the unmarked corner, back to the Root River Parkway and return to start.

I highly recommend a detour to the Boerner Botanical Gardens. Walk uphill at the intersection just after you enter Whitnall Park; here you'll see a sign for the gardens. On the way, notice the grove of conifers that covers the hillside to the right. This forest is part of a 40-acre arboretum, just a small part of the Boerner Botanical Gardens. At the top of the hill walk left toward the stone Garden Building also constructed by the Civilian Conservation Corps.

If you come to the gardens in May, you'll see thousands of tulips, daffodils and jonquils in full bloom. You might also see some early iris and the start of the extensive annual and perennial gardens.

In addition to bulb, annual and perennial gardens, there's a shrub garden, formal rose gardens, experimental gardens and an extensive herb garden. There are walkways and vistas, quiet hideaways and benches, demonstration gardens and wild places, alpine rock gardens, spring wildflowers and a walkway over a bog garden.

In June the annual Rose Festival draws thousands of enthusiasts. This event is a nine day celebration of roses, gardens, music, dance, crafts, cooking classes, children's activities and concerts.

From the gardens retrace your steps back to start.

A River Hills Ramble

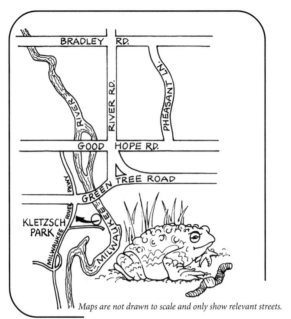

Maps are not drawn to scale and only show relevant streets.

Distance - 4.5 miles

HIGHLIGHTS

Kletzsch Park, and a glimpse of several luxurious homes

WHERE TO PARK

Kletzsch Park Picnic Areas #5-6-7

HOW TO THE THERE

Interstate 43 north to Silver Spring, west on Silver Spring to Milwaukee River Parkway, north on the parkway, turn into Kletzsch Park at the signs for Picnic Areas 3-4-5-6-7. Drive past 3 and 4 into the woods to 5-6-7.

THE ROUTE

Leave the park the way you came in. Turn right on the parkway and right again on Green Tree Road. Cross the river and turn left on River Road. North on River Road across Good Hope Road to Bradley Road. East on Bradley, south on Pheasant Lane, west on Good Hope back to River Road and retrace route back to start.

*Y*ou might want to bring a picnic and spend some time exploring this beautiful section of Kletzsch Park in Glendale. Glendale incorporated in 1950, after lengthy discussions that began in 1926. The incorporation process took so long because Glendale's southern end contained an industrial area that Milwaukee wanted. Eventually Glendale doubled its land area, striking a balance between industrial and residential neighborhoods.

The lot where you parked was once an Indian village and hidden somewhere in these woods are Indian burial grounds. You might not recognize the burial grounds but when you examine the landscape, you will see many signs of earthworm activity in the soil in the woods. These unsung heroes chomp on dirt while burrowing through the earth, sometimes down as far as two feet. As they dig they swallow soil, thus the bumps on top of the ground were left behind by hard-working worms. Dig and you'll find them. For the curious, bring a magnifying lens and examine a worm. You'll see multiple segments and the worm's contracting and relaxing muscle movements in each segment as it moves. This forward movement is assisted by retractable bristles, four pairs in each segment. With a good hand lens, one can actually see these bristles.

If you're lucky you might also spot a toad. You'll know it's a toad and not a frog if it has short legs, rough dry skin, warts and it's ugly. That is "ugly" compared to a shiny, high-jumping frog. But toads deserve our respect, for an adult can eat up to 10,000 insects in a summer and like similarly unattractive worms, toads are hard workers.

After you leave Kletzsch Park and cross Good Hope Road, you'll enter River Hills, incorporated in 1930. This suburb will always have a small population relative to its area, as the original zoning laws mandated five-acre home sites.

This part of the walk is a ramble past some of Milwaukee's most spectacular homes, or might I suggest, estates. They're surrounded by manicured lawns and in most cases a tasteful "green line" between the home and the road. Occasionally there's more than a green line and all that's visible from the street is a disappearing driveway. Stylistically the homes are eclectic, as are the shrub gardens, the carefully pruned trees, the creative flower beds and the immaculate weed-free lawns. Yellow *Wall Street Journal* receptacles suggest the political leanings of the River Hills neighborhood residents.

The streets are quiet. There's no reason for through traffic because Pheasant Lane doesn't go anywhere. The absence of sidewalks means one must walk in the street, but here this practice does not present a problem.

When you leave River Hills, take Good Hope (carefully) back to River Road and retrace your steps to Kletzsch Park and start.

Milwaukee River Parkway

The old Town of Milwaukee named this parkway along the Milwaukee River in 1940. Whether the name Milwaukee was first used for the river, or for the place it led to, is not known. Evidence that it may have been used for the city can be found in the meaning of the word, "fine or good land." But the term "land" here could be more general and mean the good land of the river.

Sculpture East of the River

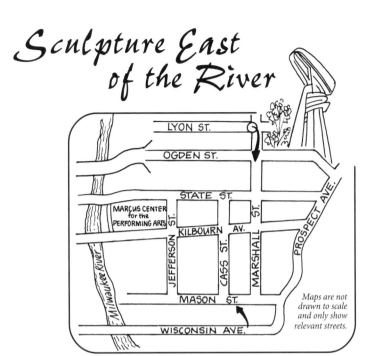

Maps are not drawn to scale and only show relevant streets.

Distance - 2 miles

HIGHLIGHTS
A visual feast of outdoor sculpture

WHERE TO PARK
At the corner of North Marshall and East Lyon Streets

HOW TO GET THERE
Take the Broadway exit off Interstate 43 just north of downtown and follow the freeway all the way to the end where it drops you off at Pick and Save. Go north ½ block and turn east on Lyon, continue to Marshall.

THE ROUTE
South on Marshall to Ogden Street. East on Ogden to Prospect Avenue. South on Prospect to Wisconsin Avenue, west on Wisconsin, then north through the Northwestern Mutual Life Insurance Company to Cass Street. West on Mason to Jefferson Street, north on Jefferson, west on Kilbourn Avenue and around the west side of the Marcus Center for the Performing Arts by the Milwaukee River. East on State Street to Marshall, north on Marshall to start.

*I*n 1995 Diane Buck and Virginia Palmer wrote *Outdoor Sculpture in Milwaukee, A Cultural and Historical Guidebook*. All I've done for this walk and the "Sculpture West of the River" walk is take a logical route through downtown Milwaukee that lets you view most of these art works in one organized outing. For more detailed information about the sculptures, consult the above book, published by the State Historical Society of Wisconsin. This is a "walk by" rather than a detailed description of each work, since otherwise this text would be too cumbersome. I hope to pique your interest, so you can go farther on your own if you wish.

Start at the corner of Marshall and Lyon with "Boy with Goose." It's in the fenced area, an oasis inside a small park near a group of Lower East Side condos. The sculpture is a replica of a statue commissioned by a private resident in 1925. Since other citizens liked it, a group of Milwaukeeans raised $800 to have a second "Boy with Goose" cast in Bremen, Germany and placed in Lake Park. Vandalized in 1964, the statue was recently moved to this location. While you're here, enjoy the fountain, the benches, and if you're inclined, bring checkers for a game on one of the game tables.

This park looks like a private area for the adjacent condos. It's not, although opening the gate presents a challenge. Since many people walk their dogs in this enclosed area, the lock system is designed to keep the dogs inside the fence.

Now walk south on Marshall and turn east on Ogden. Notice the B.C. Art Gallery with its collection of African Art and Fairchild's Cafe at the corner of Astor and Ogden Streets. You won't find a better latte in Milwaukee and Fairchild's Italian-style sandwiches, a.k.a. panini, are very good.

Continue east to Prospect Avenue and soon you'll come to the Holocaust Memorial at the Jewish Federation, 1360 Prospect. This memorial, by Claire Lieberman (1983), is designed so the viewer can walk into it and experience it in a personal way. The abstract composition is meant to stimulate questions in the mind of the viewer.

Next you'll come to the Robert Burns likeness at Burns Square, actually a triangle. The piece was cast in Edinburgh and shipped to Milwaukee in 1909. The artist is William Grant Stevenson, a famous Scottish sculptor.

When you reach Juneau Park, follow the path to the east to "Leif, the Discoverer" (1887) by sculptor Anne Whitney. He's shown here, larger than life, looking out to sea. Farther south in Juneau Park look for the likeness of Solomon Juneau (1888), standing in his buckskin suit, rifle in his hand, looking out over land that would soon become Milwaukee.

Solomon Juneau, Milwaukee's first mayor, came here in 1818 as an agent for the American Fur Company. He knew how to pick real estate when he chose the best land at the confluence of the Milwaukee, Menomonee and Kinnickinnic Rivers. Placement of his likeness in this park is appropriate since Juneau Park was Milwaukee's first public park.

At the south end of Juneau Park, if you look toward Lake Michigan you'll see "Delicate Balance," "Calipers" and "Monumental Holistic III" described in the "Along the Lakefront" walk. As you follow Prospect around to the front of the Milwaukee Art Museum you'll pass the Abraham Lincoln sculpture, the World War I Memorial flagpole and "The Calling." These sculptures were also described in "Along the Lakefront."

Walk west on Wisconsin Avenue and turn into the small park at Northwestern Mutual Life Insurance Company. This little jewel has layers of fountains and waterfalls with horizontal and vertical blocks of stone creating cascades of flowing water that capture the essence of rocky waterfalls in the mountains, where several streams come together and create a sensory feast of splashing water. On a windy day, feel the spray. On a sunny day, look for a rainbow.

Follow Mason west to Jefferson, turn north and walk one block to Cathedral Square. Here you'll find two sculptures, "Immigrant Mother" (1960) and "Tulip Fountain" (1969). Both are self-explanatory in shape and design.

Hungry? Across the street on Jefferson at Louise's Trattoria the chefs make a fine calzone and fantastic bread to dip in rosemary-scented olive oil. Next door the DeLind Fine Art Gallery is well worth a stop especially since this is an "art" walk.

Turn west on Kilbourn Avenue and look for "The Great Double" (1972), at the MGIC Plaza. When this piece was commissioned for the plaza, the space was redesigned so the sculpture would give viewers the impression of space and monumentality. The curved lines of this abstract work contrast with the geometric lines of the building behind it.

As you walk west on Kilbourn you'll come to the Marcus Center for the Performing Arts. The statue "Trigon" on the grounds of the center is a composition representing music, dance and theater. This fascinating piece changes character as one views it from different angles or as the light changes during the day.

The last sculpture on this walk is "Laureate" (1969), by Seymour Lipton, commissioned by the Allen-Bradley Company, and dedicated to their founder Harry Lynde Bradley. Sculptor Lipton created a piece that illustrates man's heroic nature and the struggle of human existence in a highly personal expressionistic distortion of the human figure. During the dedication ceremonies Lipton said he was invariably drawn to the best examples of primitive art and "selected forms to intensify the human metaphor."

With these lofty ideals I conclude the walk. Follow State back to Marshall and walk north on Marshall back to start.

Sculpture West of the River

MacARTHUR SQUARE

COURTHOUSE

KILBOURN AV.

WELLS ST.

WISCONSIN AV.

2nd ST.

5th ST.

7th

10th ST.

Maps are not drawn to scale and only show relevant streets.

MILWAUKEE

Distance - 2 miles

HIGHLIGHTS
  Outdoor sculpture

WHERE TO PARK
  At the corner of 5th Street and Kilbourn Avenue

HOW TO GET THERE
  Take Interstate 43 north; just past the Marquette Interchange, take the Civic Center / Kilbourn exit and follow Kilbourn east to 5th Street.

THE ROUTE
  East on Kilbourn to 2nd Street, south on 2nd to Wisconsin Avenue, west on Wisconsin to 10th Street. North one block on 10th and east on Wells Street to 7th Street, north on 7th to Kilbourn and east on Kilbourn to start.

Walk east on Kilbourn Avenue entering the area in downtown Milwaukee where out-of-towners gather. They'll visit places such as the Convention Center at 4th Street, the Bradley Center a block north on 4th, the Hyatt, Polaris Restaurant, and Major Goolsby's Bar and Grill. On a weekday morning, this intersection is deserted, quite unlike a night or a weekend when there's an event at the Bradley Center.

At Old World Third Street take a short detour to see the gargoyles on a stone fence. They represent a musician, the town crier, a photographer, a printer, a writer, an electronic communicator and a telephone operator. Each has its own humorous personality, capturing sculptor Dick Wilkin's sense of whimsy. These sprites represent employees of Milwaukee newspapers. Done in 1969, they're a quaint reminder of the way a daily newspaper was produced before the advent of electronic communications and the Internet.

Return to Kilbourn and follow it past the Milwaukee County Historical Society, 910 North Old World Third Street. This building, built in 1911, was originally the Second Ward Savings Bank. The last owner, The First Wisconsin National Bank, donated it to the county in 1965 for use as a museum.

Next you'll come to Pere Marquette Park, dedicated to the memory of Father Jacques Marquette and Sieur Louis Joliet, the first known white men to visit this site, in 1674. From this park you can walk down to the Milwaukee River and enjoy a section of the Milwaukee River Walk, still under construction when this book was published.

Back on Kilbourn, turn right briefly on Plankinton Avenue and angle right or south to 2nd Street where you'll see the "Letter Carrier's Monument" (1932), at the intersection of 2nd, Wells and Plankinton. The artist, Elliot Offner sculpted three carriers, two men and a woman. He intended to symbolize the dignity and diversity of all letter carriers. Don't miss this often-overlooked sculpture, dwarfed by the hubbub of downtown Milwaukee.

Follow 2nd to Wisconsin Avenue and turn west. After one

block you'll come to "Family" (1983), an abstract work by Helaine Blumenfeld located in front of the Henry Reuss Federal Building. The artist personally selected sixty-eight tons of granite to be transported to her studio in Carrara, Italy, where she and four assistants worked on the final piece, which weighs a mere thirty-eight tons.

At 818 Wisconsin you'll see a treasure, the Milwaukee Public Library. Constructed in 1893, this fine example of Classical Revival architecture was the winning design in a national competition. Notice the Italian Renaissance ornamental features. Walk inside to view the rotunda, elegant all the way from its mosaic floor to its elaborate dome.

Next you'll come to four important sculptures known as the "Court of Honor." The first, a bronze representation of George Washington was given to the city in 1885 by Elizabeth Plankinton. Next, a soldier holding a rifle commemorates all those who fought in the war with Spain. Placed here in 1932, it's entitled simply "Spanish-American War Soldier." The artist was Ferdinand Koenig. The third piece, "Midsummer Carnival Shaft" (1900), is a sixty-five foot column with a sphere on top in honor of a carnival held on this site from 1898 to 1901. Perhaps this carnival was Milwaukee's first Summerfest. The last piece is an 1898 Civil War grouping of four soldiers by John S. Conway. Entitled "The Victorious Charge," this piece captures a moment in battle with great intensity and realism.

Between 9th and 10th Streets, the elegant private Wisconsin Club is part of the original residence of an early settler, Alexander Mitchell. Once a humble house on a small lot, it grew in stages to become an imposing mansion that encompassed an entire block. The scroll-cut eight-sided summer house, built in 1871, looks like the gingerbread house where the wicked witch from *Hansel and Gretel* might have lived.

Walk into the Wisconsin Club if it's open. Since it's available for private parties, sometimes they'll show guests around the interior. It's a splendid example of old wood and leather in a manly setting where just a hint of cigar scents the parlor.

Walk north on 10th Street to Wells and Clas Park, the Milwaukee County Courthouse and the fountain "Solidarity / The Spirit of Polonia" (1969) by Edmund Lewandowski. The fountain was commissioned by the Polish Women's Cultural Club in honor of Polanki, the radical Polish trade union movement.

As you walk east on Wells past the Milwaukee Public Museum you'll pass "Woodland Indian" and "Whistling Swans" by Marshall Fredericks. This work has become associated with the mission of the museum, to teach and to preserve natural and human history.

The next sculpture is hard to find. Go back on Wells and just before you get to the museum, turn north to MacArthur Square to visit the General. The family of General Douglas MacArthur has roots in Milwaukee so it's appropriate to erect his likeness here on the Civic Center Plaza. This piece, created by Robert Dean, dates to 1979.

From here you can walk down the steps to Kilbourn Avenue and east to the last sculpture on this route, "Referee"(1978) by Tom Queoff, located at the south entrance to the Arena. It's a product of the federally funded Comprehensive Employment and Training Act (CETA), active in Milwaukee from 1977-1981. One of CETA's goals was to give trained artists a chance to work in the community. "Referee" is made of travertine marble slabs, leftovers from the construction of the First Wisconsin Bank building, laminated together by artist Queoff.

On March 3, 1997, the Rock Bottom Restaurant and Brewery opened next to the Milwaukee River at 740 North Plankinton. You walked past it. I unconditionally recommend a stop here for a sandwich, a salad, or a veggie enchilada. On Friday, they serve a fish and chips dinner with salmon instead of perch or cod. You'll also want to try a freshly brewed ale. What could taste better on a warm summer evening than a cold beer on the patio, a brewer's club sandwich with chipotle mayonnaise and an enormous piece of carrot cake with cream cheese frosting sitting in a pool of luscious caramel sauce?

A Serendipitous Adventure

Maps are not drawn to scale and only show relevant streets.

Distance - 3.5 miles

HIGHLIGHTS
Bay View, a secluded beach walk, St. Francis Seminary, Seminary Woods, solitude and spring wildflowers

WHERE TO PARK
Close to the artesian well in the 1700 block of East Pryor Avenue. If you wish, bring containers to fill at the well.

HOW TO GET THERE
South on Interstate 94 to the Lincoln / Becher exit. East on Lincoln Avenue to Logan Street. South on Logan to Conway Street, east on Conway to Superior Street. South on Superior to Pryor Avenue.

THE ROUTE
Walk east on Pryor to Superior Street. Detour a block north, then

*follow Superior south to the beach and boat launch at Nock Street,
then follow the path along Lake Michigan to where it goes uphill back
to Superior. Walk northwest on Superior to the entrance to St. Francis
Seminary and walk west through the Seminary grounds (with three
detours into the woods). Follow the service road and keep turning
right past a parking lot until the route comes out on Illinois Avenue.
Follow Illinois to Oklahoma, east on Oklahoma one block to Superior
and north on Superior back to start.*

Since I had a grand adventure putting this route together,
I have no doubt anyone who follows it will have a similar
experience. The directions to Seminary Woods alone are worth
the price of this book, for if I counted the number of false starts
I made, I would need both hands. You'll learn more about this
later in the walk.

The route starts and ends in Bay View, originally a company
town built around the Milwaukee Iron Works, an iron and steel
mill. The town was made up of small workers' cottages, taverns,
churches and a yacht club. Homes built here date to the 1870s,
encompassing a wide range of architectural styles that reflect
the late 1800s through the mid 1900s.

People who live here tend to think of it as a city-within-a-
city, while many outsiders consider Bay View just another
south-of-downtown Milwaukee suburb. Actually, it's neither,
for Bay View has been part of the City of Milwaukee since 1887.

Start this walk at the artesian well on Pryor Avenue. This is
the only artesian well still functioning and approved by the City
Health Department, whose employees check it every two
months. Since its source is deep, and it draws pure water from
many miles distant, feel free to imbibe. Do bring bottles to fill;
everyone does. Weekend mornings bring many health-con-
scious locals to the well with bottles to fill with this good pure
water. In summertime someone plants flowers by the well; the
city has added sitting benches.

Walk east to Superior Street and take a one block detour to
see two distinguished homes. The first, at 2582, stands out

because it's far more lavish than the surrounding cottages, built for workers at the steel mill. Joseph Starkey, superintendent of the North Chicago Rolling Mills, lived in this luxurious home. Another executive home at 2590 was the Warren Brinton residence, built in 1871 by mechanics from the Bay View Rolling Mills, where Mr. Brinton was their superintendent.

Walk back on Superior Street to Nock and go directly to Lake Michigan. You're standing at the north end of South Shore Park; to the left is the South Shore Yacht Club. This club got its start in 1913 in the lakefront home of William Barr and met there until the present clubhouse was built in 1936.

Walk through the parking lot past the fish cleaning tables and the park administration building, and follow the asphalt path that parallels the lake for about a quarter of a mile. When the trail forks to the right, stay down by the lake. I especially enjoy this area because the view of Milwaukee can't be beat, and few walkers come here to see it. It's a good walk in both directions with either the skyline or infinite blue water in sight along the deserted beach.

After you pass wooden steps you'll come to a place where the path leaves the beach. Follow the path uphill and walk across the grass to Superior Street. You began in South Shore Park and exited from Bay View Park.

Walk back on Superior Street to St. Francis Seminary, then enter the lovely tree-shaded avenue that leads to Henni Hall. One could be in France instead of Milwaukee, strolling beneath a canopy of meticulously pruned sugar maple trees.

Now you've come to the part of the walk that will eventually take you into Seminary Woods. My first false start came just before the formal entrance to Henni Hall where a trail leads behind a pair of stone pillars and a sign reads "No vehicles beyond this point." Walk in here and follow the road / trail to a turnaround where a second sign reads, "Seminary Woods Wildlife Preserve endorsed by Milwaukee Audobon Society protected by state and federal laws." At this point, I thought I was in Seminary

Woods, but I was wrong. However this little private corner seems a likely place for solitude and spring blooms.

When you come out of the woods, Henni Hall is straight ahead. It was built in 1855-56 of cream city brick, made on the spot by the Brothers of St. Francis. While the brothers worked, the sisters cooked for them. This Italianate building is lovely, as are the grounds and the views of Lake Michigan. Inside Henni Hall are the administrative offices for the seminary, founded in 1845 by John Martin Henni, who envisioned an educational institution to prepare young men to be priests for German-speaking Catholics throughout the United States.

Martin Henni, the first Bishop of Milwaukee, purchased this land for a seminary in 1853. The property was once an Indian village called Njoshing, meaning "a strip of land jutting out into the water." Just to the left of Henni Hall is the archbishop's residence. Notice the sign by the parking area, "Thou shalt not park here."

On the north side of Henni Hall, hidden behind tennis courts gone to seed, another trail enters another woods. This trail was the second false start in my quest for the bona fide Seminary Woods. Instead, I found a magical maple-beech forest with nearly 100% shade cover on a hot summer day. I'd expect to find a carpet of wildflowers here in May before the dense canopy shuts out the sun and cools the soil.

The best way to exit these woods is to retrace your steps to the tennis courts. Now, walk to the south side of the complex, past the bishop's residence and a line of five garage doors until you see a wide path leading into the woods about one hundred yards beyond Henni Hall. Follow this path into the authentic Seminary Woods. Here I turn you loose in the woods with the assurance you'll be able to find you way back to the entrance. Be sure to walk far enough into the woods to find the cemetery, where several dozen grave markers suggest an epidemic must have swept through the seminary in the late 1800s. As you walk to the cemetery, you'll see a network of paths to explore.

After you've found your way out of the woods, follow the service road and turn right at the sign for the Vocation Office, until you come to a road that will take you to Illinois Street. Turn right on Illinois, right on Oklahoma, left or northwest on Superior and return to start.

If you're hungry after all this adventure, stop for a meal at Wagner's Bookstore and Cafe at the corner of Oklahoma and Delaware. Breakfasts feature omelets, Lizz's croissant, great muffins, morning buns from La Boulangerie and good strong coffee. If it's a hot day, enjoy an ice cream cone or a cold soda and perhaps one of their delicious sandwiches.

Pryor Avenue

William J. and Elizabeth Pryor, who were Bay View residents at the time, platted this street in 1872. When William died in 1876 at the age of 52, the Pryor family moved back to Waupun, Wisconsin.

Pryor Avenue is the site of Milwaukee's only public well. The well, opened a few years after Pryor's death, has been a public source of water ever since. Over the years, legends and theories about the water's origins and properties have abounded. But the fact is that the water flows from Waukesha County and contains no special ingredients; just iron, calcium and fluorine.

A Trip Back Into Time

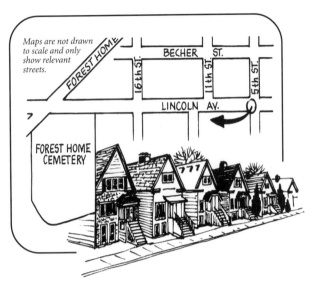

Maps are not drawn to scale and only show relevant streets.

FOREST HOME

BECHER ST.

16th St.

11th St.

5th St.

LINCOLN AV.

FOREST HOME CEMETERY

Distance - 4 miles

HIGHLIGHTS
> Lincoln Avenue, Forest Home Cemetery and rows of Polish flats

WHERE TO PARK
> Corner of 5th Street and Lincoln Avenue

HOW TO GET THERE
> South on Interstate 94 to the Lincoln/Becher exit. Cross Becher and continue south to Lincoln Avenue.

THE ROUTE
> West on Lincoln to Forest Home Cemetery; enter at the intersection of West Forest Home Avenue and Lincoln Avenue, check map on page 75 for directions inside the cemetery. Return to Lincoln and walk east to 16th Street, north on 16th to Becher Street, east on Becher to 11th Street, south on 11th to Lincoln and back to start.

*G*et an early start for this south side tour and don't be in a hurry. There's a lot to see and once you're inside Forest Home Cemetery you'll want time to meander.

The first landmark on the walk is St. Josaphat Basilica at 5th and Lincoln. Milwaukee's most richly decorated church was constructed from 1897 to 1901 using materials salvaged from the Chicago Post Office. Pastor, Father Grutza purchased a five hundred-car trainload of limestone blocks, marble, granite columns and woodwork for $20,000. The church was designated a Basilica in 1929 by Pope Pius XI, the third church in the country to receive that honor.

I chose this walk because I'm fascinated with the ethnicity of Lincoln Avenue from 5th Street to Forest Home Cemetery. It's easy to drive down these few blocks, seeing just the uninteresting first floors of the buildings, but if you look up, you'll see an architectural treasure, buildings that reflect a European tradition dating back to the Middle Ages.

Around 1900 residential development in this area began to increase and Lincoln became a commercial strip where residents could purchase household needs, visit a tavern or see a movie. Unlike Mitchell Street to the north where large professional buildings, such as banks, offices and department stores were located, this was a neighborhood shopping district.

On Lincoln, merchants lived in apartments above their shops, demonstrating their status and prestige by the degree of ornamentation on their street-facing gables. Stepped gables, resembling those of the 13th century, gradually evolved with the addition of scrolls, pediments and classical details. Originally a German form, stepped gables were adopted by Milwaukee's Polish community, perhaps as a visual status symbol to working-class Poles.

As you travel west to 24th Street and the cemetery, take note of these historic buildings, built or remodeled into their present forms between 1910 and 1920. Many of the merchants began with simple frame buildings that they replaced when they could with brick, a building material denoting status.

The first two stops on this walk are not about German or

Polish architecture. On the northeast corner of Lincoln and 7th Avenue, is Lincoln Avenue Pottery, a fine place to shop for hand-made ceramic pieces, both functional and decorative. The storefront showcases local potters as well as well-known ceramic artists from around the Midwest and beyond.

The second stop is the statue of General Thaddeus Kosciuszko (1905) in the park named after him. This fifteen foot-tall bronze equestrian was done by Gaetano Trentanove to commemorate Kosciuszko's contribution to the success of the Americans during the Revolutionary War. Trentanove received $13,000 for this commission, taking a year to create the statue in his studio in Florence, Italy. The seven ton statue sits on a granite pedestal designed by prolific Milwaukee architects Ferry and Clas.

Start the "Lincoln Avenue parade of Polish shopkeepers" at 501, a building with a sign that says "Doctor's Denture Systems," originally a pharmacy and drug store until the 1960s.

The locksmith and hardware store at 604 was built in 1898, the buildings at 608, 610 and 612 in 1899. They illustrate Baroque Revival architecture, with its use of rounded forms. Some say that Father Grutza, Pastor of St. Josaphat's across the street, had these buildings built with leftover materials from the church. Notice the sharp contrast between the street-level storefronts and the architectural details on the 2nd floors. You'll see this juxtaposition of the 1900s and the 1990s all along Lincoln Avenue.

At 1033 the Krzewinski Building, built in 1907, is an example of a simple stepped profile without any additional ornamentation. At 1112 the Bzdawka Building, built in 1919, has a handsome combination of steps and curves in the gable with a large keystone at the crest. This was originally a butcher shop in a plain wood building. When Bzdawka took over the shop in 1919, he replaced the simple shop with this impressive brick structure.

In the next block you might want to pay a visit to A.J. Polish

Deli, Milwaukee's only Polish grocery store.

At 1530 look above the Lincoln Super Market to the dramatic gables that face both Lincoln and 15th Street. This corner commercial building with four upstairs flats is one of Lincoln Avenue's landmark buildings.

Don't miss Lopez Bakery at the corner of Lincoln and 16th Street. The Lopez family has owned a bakery at the corner of 6th and National Avenue for many years and this location is a second site for this outstanding bakery. Owner Jose Lopez brought family recipes with him when he came to Milwaukee from the state of Jalisco. There isn't a better bakery in town!

Farther west between 20th and 21st streets notice the solid block of Polish flats, an architectural phenomenon unique to Milwaukee. Built primarily by people of Polish descent, these homes typically started as small frame cottages set on cedar post foundations. As families grew and relatives arrived from Europe, the Poles literally lifted their wooden houses and added partially raised basement apartments beneath the original structures.

These basement apartments, built of wood, brick or concrete block, had street-level windows and outside entrances. Steep wooden steps leading to a small porch at the entrance would be added to the upper units. This way a family could grow and expand, as home-improvement projects were more economical than moving to a new home. Of equal importance, Polish people have strong attachments to home, neighborhood and church.

Continue west on Lincoln to Forest Home Avenue and the cemetery. Inside the cemetery, the Hall of History is a fascinating museum with photographs and biographical information about Milwaukee's early settlers. Here are restrooms, a bubbler and chairs to sit in while contemplating this quiet dignified museum.

After leaving the museum, follow the map to two sculptures, both in section 33. The first is the T.A. Chapman Memorial, done in 1896 by Daniel Chester French. Chapman, who came to Milwaukee in 1856 and died in 1892, ran a well-respected dry-goods store. His widow Laura and their two daughters chose the best-known sculptor of the time to create his memorial. Daniel Chester French, famous for his angels, sculpted this small angel holding an unidentified container.

Nearby, the William A. Starke Memorial was done in 1921 by another nationally known artist, Robert Ingersoll Aitken. This bronze, another angel done with bold classical symbols, differs stylistically from the Chapman Memorial. It's interesting to compare them and to note the differences.

To locate these two angels, use the grave markers for Borchard, Pieper, Vance and Hilty as landmarks. It helps to know the Chapman and Starke Memorials have their backs to each other.

After you leave the Forest Home Cemetery, walk east on Lincoln to 16th Street and north on 16th to 2221 and a residence built in 1857 by Carl Kunckell. This beautiful Italianate home has a cream city brick tower standing a full story above the roof line. The original six acre property has been reduced to a small lot supported by a retaining wall.

Turn east on Becher Street and come to the Church Ecclesia St. Hyacinth and a statue of St. Hyacinth. The rectory next door is a classic cream city brick residence hiding behind two blue spruce trees.

When you come to 13th Street, take a short detour to 2074 to see a Polish flat that was built in 1900 for $2000. This one's a little different from the flats you passed on Lincoln Avenue, since the owner included the raised basement as an original feature rather than adding it later. Furthermore it's built of cream city brick, suggesting that the family was prosperous.

Continue east on Becher to 11th Street. Take 11th south to Lincoln and return to start. On the southwest corner Tio Beta's, a small unpretentious Mexican restaurant, has excellent food. Owner and chef Alberto Guzman came to Milwaukee from

Zacatecas in the state of Guanajuato. Everything tastes good especially camarones ranchero, ten succulent shrimp in a red sauce; flautas, corn tortillas filled with chicken and deep fried; and flan, a rich baked custard dessert coated with caramel sauce. If it's a weekend, come in the morning for huevos rancheros. I can't think of a better way to begin or end this leisurely stroll through history.

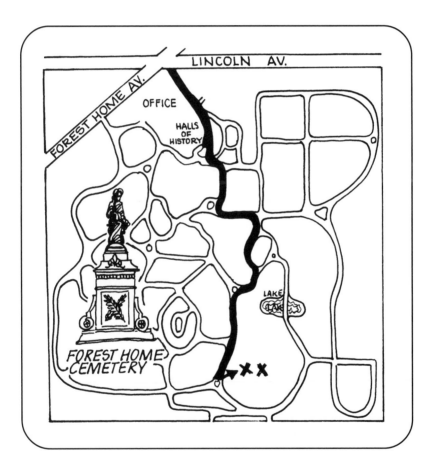

Two Formerly Elegant Streets

MCKINLEY BLVD.

35th ST.

27th ST.

HIGHLAND BLVD.

STATE ST.

Maps are not drawn to scale and only show relevant streets.

Distance - 1.5 miles

HIGHLIGHTS

Cold Spring Park and Sauerkraut Boulevard, once prosperous neighborhoods settled by wealthy German immigrants

WHERE TO PARK

At the corner of 27th Street and State Street

HOW TO GET THERE

Interstate 94 west to 35th Street. North on 35th to State Street. East on State to 27th Street.

THE ROUTE

North on 27th Street to Highland Boulevard, west on Highland to 35th Street. North on 35th to McKinley Boulevard, east on McKinley to 27th and back to State Street.

*I*n the mid-1800s, Highland Boulevard went west only as far as 12th Street. In 1876, Highland was extended to 27th Street and after 1890, Highland between 27th and 35th Streets became an elegant residential neighborhood. The Pabst family, the Miller family and the Usinger family, still familiar to us in 1997, built homes on this prosperous boulevard. Since those families, plus several other well-to-do German families, all located on Highland within a few blocks, the street earned the nickname "Sauerkraut Boulevard." That's the first part of this walk.

The second part will take you to McKinley Boulevard, once the site of the sixty-acre Cold Spring Park race track. It took its name from a natural spring in the northwest corner of the grounds. Later the track was used for a Civil War encampment, Camp Washburn, and finally, for just one year, the site was used for the Wisconsin State Fair. Today this neighborhood is known as Cold Spring Park and the area has been designated a historic district by the Milwaukee Historical Society.

This background may help explain the development of these two adjacent neighborhoods. From 1890 to 1910 Milwaukee's population increased dramatically and new housing was needed. These two West Side streets, Highland and McKinley, became highly desirable residential locations although they attracted different income groups. Wealthy industrialists and beer barons were drawn to Highland while professional and managerial classes settled on McKinley. Both groups were primarily German-American. The neighborhood between them, less prestigious, was settled by managers, craftspeople and laborers.

Now the walk. Start from 27th and State with a short detour to see a home at 3011 State. Set back from State Street, it once fronted on Watertown Plank Road. The home was built in 1850 by Robert Faries, Wisconsin's first dentist. Faries is also remembered because he built the first telescope in the state.

At 2710 State, Colonel Theodore Yates built a "country home," actually more like an estate. Today it's boarded up.

There's a sense of former elegance in these homes built in the late 1800s and it's sad to see their disintegration on this tree-lined street.

At the corner of 27th and Highland, Saint Luke Emanuel Baptist Church, built in 1913, is patterned after the Pantheon in Rome. Notice the porticos in front of a domed roof.

As you walk west on Highland you'll come to the Gettelman home at 2929. Farther down the Boulevard, the Frederick Pabst Jr. residence at 3112 was one of the first six mansions built here. The four Ionic columns, each made from a single block of limestone with a slight curve in the middle, made this quite a showplace. At 3209 the George Koch home, also built in 1897, has often been mistaken for a library. The classical balustrades and columns give it an impressive entrance. Add stone lions and it looks more like a public building than a private residence. Concordia College owns the building though the college has moved to the suburbs.

In one hundred-plus years, Sauerkraut Boulevard, today known as Highland Boulevard, has deteriorated. The population moved out of the neighborhood toward the north and west, leading to an inevitable decay. Although it's sad to see this decline, there's hope that perhaps someday this process will be reversed, and these magnificent homes will be restored and converted to condos or apartments.

Highland Avenue, Boulevard
Highland Boulevard was created from Edward Holton's farm, "Highland Home." It was subdivided by the Highland Home Land Company in 1887.

When you come to 35th Street, turn north and then east on McKinley. You've left Sauerkraut and entered the heart of Cold Spring Park, less affluent but no less fascinating. This tree-lined boulevard showcases eight blocks of turn-of-the-century historic homes.

The home at 3317, built before 1915, is typical of the tract homes that were built in the 3200 and 3300 blocks. The floor plans of these homes are similar, however owners and builders individualized the exteriors. This row of homes is a good example of hundreds, maybe thousands of three-story frame duplexes built in central Milwaukee.

At 3112, architect Herman Buemming designed a house that is almost identical to his home on Pleasant Street. (See Yankee Hill South walk.) Both have Ionic columns, but the pronounced dentil moldings on this home give it a Georgian look while the home on Pleasant Street looks more Greek.

At 3102, the home built in 1904 for the George Zimmerman family cost approximately $6500. Notice the dormers facing the street.

Two blocks farther down McKinley is a home that's typical of those built by upper-middle class Germans. They were often made of brick and had lofty gables, occasionally with half-timbering facing the street. They had stone porches and closely resembled homes built in Germany at the turn of the century. More of these homes can be seen at 3120, 3003, 2902 and 2801 McKinley.

Of the two boulevards, Highland and McKinley, I found McKinley more interesting, perhaps because it comes closer to retaining its original character. Highland is a major east-west artery and the combination of traffic and boxy commercial buildings has diluted its original character.

Nevertheless this is an interesting walk. Sauerkraut Boulevard and Cold Spring Park are part of Milwaukee's history and researching this walk took me on foot into a part of town where I would not have thought to take a Saturday stroll.

A Visit to Grant Park

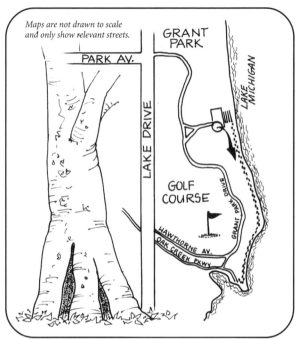

Maps are not drawn to scale and only show relevant streets.

PARK AV.

GRANT PARK

LAKE MICHIGAN

LAKE DRIVE

GOLF COURSE

GRANT PARK DRIVE

HAWTHORNE AV.

OAK CREEK PKWY.

Distance - 3 miles

HIGHLIGHTS
   Grant Park, the Seven Bridges Trail and a secluded Lake Michigan beach

WHERE TO PARK
   In the parking lot for the Seven Bridges Trail

HOW TO GET THERE
   South on Interstate 94 to College Avenue, east on College to Chicago Avenue and south on Chicago to Park Avenue. East on Park into Grant Park. Follow the park drive south to the parking lot for the Seven Bridges Trail.

THE ROUTE
   Start at the bridge across the ravine, turn left at the first intersection and left again on the trail that parallels the ravine. At the "dedication"

*sign walk straight toward Lake Michigan and keep bearing right on
the trail that follows the lake. At picnic area #2 pick up the path and
follow it to the golf course. Walk south to Oak Creek Parkway.
Turn left down the hill and walk to the beach. Follow the beach back
to steps that lead uphill. Take a sharp right and return to start.*

*T*he Seven Bridges Trail was built in the 1930s by the
Civilian Conservation Corps. A crew of two hundred men
constructed retaining walls, staircases and lannon stone paths.
From the 1930s to the 1960s, this trail, cutting across ravines
and through a mature forest, was a romantic destination for
young and old.

More recently, budget cuts meant less money was available
to maintain the original trails in county parks. Fortunately the
county got a grant in 1995 to hire the Wisconsin Conservation
Corps to rebuild the Seven Bridges Trail. The Corps trains
young unemployed men and women in conservation-related
fields. In July 1995, work began on this trail and a formal
dedication took place on July 21, l996.

When you enter, a sign on the bridge across the ravine
reads, "Enter this wild wood and view the haunts of nature." Be
sure to notice the mature beech trees along this first section of
the trail. Beech trees have smooth gray bark that resembles an
elephant's sturdy leg. This stand of beech trees is one of the few
left in southeastern Wisconsin.

The surrounding ravines were planted in the 1920s to
attract birds in the hope the ravines would become a bird
sanctuary. The conifers reflect the German influence and in
fact, some of the Norway spruce were started from seedlings
collected in the Black Forest of Germany.

These woods also contain many native Wisconsin conifers
such as red and white pine. Since the soil conditions here are
comparable to those of northern Wisconsin, these native pine
trees can thrive here in southern Wisconsin.

You'll take two left turns before you take the high road

alongside Lake Michigan. You'll know you're on the right path if you're walking south and you can see the beach below. Along the way many small private grassy areas may beckon to you. Take a few minutes to enjoy the grass, the view, the beach, a sunny day, and this park surrounded by suburbia. Marvel, as I do, at the foresight of the men and women who set this lakefront aside for park land. You could be wending your way through a forest of condos instead of following a secluded path.

Notice the signs of erosion and the natural process of water gradually altering this bluff. In fact, if parts of the bluff along this walk seem too unstable, please follow the bike trail. There are places where someone unsteady might be challenged by the narrow path and the drop-off to the beach. Where it hugs the bluff, the path might not be safe for young children.

Just beyond the place where the path tunnels through a brushy area, you'll arrive at picnic area #2. At the far end of the picnic grounds, pick up the path again just past several large birch trees. If you visit in May you'll see mayapple, trillium, Solomon's plume and the ubiquitous poison ivy.

Soon the path ends and you'll arrive at the Grant Park Golf Course. Keep walking in a southerly direction past the clubhouse to Oak Creek Parkway, then turn left and scoot down the hill to the beach.

Now it's time to wander along the beach, heading north. Feel free to take your time and to enjoy the lovely ambiance of a deserted beach. However, if Lake Michigan has a high water year, this beach walk could be under water. If this should happen, turn around and retrace the first part of this walk back to start.

When you come to the jetties, choose a table. In August 1996 I counted 12 picnic tables in various states of disrepair. Some were almost completely buried but a few remained above ground. This situation changes every spring when the ice melts.

A table will give you a front row seat to watch hundreds of gulls and their fascinating activities. The gulls, with their square or rounded tails, are impressive swimmers, floaters and standers. Their menu won't be particularly appealing but without their taste in dead fish and garbage, the beach would be littered with disgusting refuse. Don't get too close. These "sanitary workers" have very bad breath.

In August I found the base of the bluff covered with colorful but unwelcome purple loosestrife, a plant that came to Wisconsin wetlands several years ago. It's an invasive plant, which unchecked will dominate an area, crowding out all the native species. Purple loosestrife dramatically changes the habitat, so indigenous plants and animals can no longer survive there.

I hope you left your watch at home. You can't rush this walk so why try? Soft sand will slow you down, as will tiny stones not yet ground into sand. Here's a place to cultivate the saying, a favorite of mine, "There's more to life than increasing its speed."

Eventually you'll come to a wide beach. Cross a bridge and start up the newly cemented steps. Here I found youngsters doing what they've been doing since the beginning of time, building dams with rocks where the stream drains into the lake.

Climb the steps where recently cemented stones line both sides of the walk and new log railings provide a hand grip. At the top of the stairs take a sharp right and you've made a loop back to start.

Where the trail ends you'll see a sign with another park quote "May the God given peace of this leafy solitude rest upon and abide with thee."

By now you're wondering why I referred to Seven Bridges Trail since you've only crossed two bridges. I leave it to you to meander around the rest of this compact trail system and find the other five. Here's a hint: look down the ravine as you walk back to the car to see four additional bridges and if you follow the lower trail you'll also see number five.

A Wetland Wander

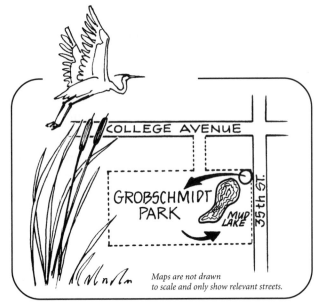

COLLEGE AVENUE

GROBSCHMIDT
PARK

MUD
LAKE

35th ST.

*Maps are not drawn
to scale and only show relevant streets.*

Distance - 1 mile

HIGHLIGHTS
  *Grobschmidt Park, a place for bird watchers and a green oasis
  surrounded by suburbia*

WHERE TO PARK
  On 35th Street at the beginning of the walk

HOW TO GET THERE
  *Interstate 94 south to College Avenue, west on College to 35th Street,
  south on 35th to the trail leading west into Grobschmidt Park.*

THE ROUTE
  Follow the foot path around Mud Lake and back to start.

Don't bring your dog on this walk or you'll have to turn
back and come another time. A prominent sign at the beginning of the walk prohibits a canine companion. Enter the park

on a wide gravel path and soon you'll see Mud Lake to the left. In summer it will be partially hidden behind a ring of tall cattails. At once, you'll feel that you've left the city behind. If you come on an August day, the path will be a green tunnel, a piece of "up north" surrounded by suburban homes, condos, apartment buildings and strip malls.

On this walk around the lake you'll notice the air smells like it does around a pond three hundred miles north of Milwaukee. Choose one of the many paths that lead to the edge of Mud Lake and you'll be rewarded by the sight of many bird species.

A great blue heron is often spotted here. Stand quietly and watch this large bird with a long neck and powerful beak, standing motionless, almost invisible, ready to spear his dinner. If you accidentally startle the heron, he'll temporarily leave his feeding area and you might see both a graceful take-off and landing.

You're also likely to see a kingfisher, an odd-looking bird with a long bill, a large head that looks too big for his body and a crest that looks as if he's having a bad hair day. He's blue-green on top and white underneath with a gray-blue belt across his chest. He'll dive for a small fish and swallow it whole.

Of course you'll see ducks, most likely mallards, as they're the ones who choose to hang around civilization. Mallards will eat almost anything including water plants, insects, old bread and stale cookie crumbs. They're equally non-discriminating about where they breed. The male is showy with a velvet-green head and neck, yellow bill and orange feet, unlike the female, who is unobtrusive except when she quacks.

You may also see geese; the largest will be the Canada goose. This large goose weighs 10 pounds or more and has a five foot wingspan. The name Canada goose, by the way, does not refer to his or her country of origin.

If you've come to walk here in May, there's a good chance you'll see migrating warblers flitting among the trees and shrubs. When they come through Milwaukee in May, the warblers are wearing their "dress-up clothes." Look carefully to see a variety of yellow, yellow-green, orange and black and orange birds, all smaller than a sparrow and without exception, shy.

Most warblers are heading farther north, except perhaps the tiny ovenbird. This species nests in the woods, but they're especially bashful so you won't be likely to see an ovenbird. However, you might have heard his loud cry, "Teacher, teacher, teacher."

Another small bird often seen here is the goldfinch. You can recognize it because in summer the male finch is the only small yellow bird with black wings and a black tail.

As you follow the path around the lake, beware of poison ivy. Three shiny notched leaves will be your signal to avoid touching this plant. It can leave you with a burning itch that goes through many stages and can last as long as three weeks.

On the far side of Mud Lake notice the prairie plants including prairie dock, purple and yellow coneflower and the tall cup plant with its square stem.

At the end of the path you'll come out to the road at Parkwood Village, a group of luxury townhouses. Turn left and return to start.

It occurred to me after I took this walk how pleasant it would be to come here on a summer evening with a folding chair. I'd find a good place to watch the activity around the edge of Mud Lake, sit back, lose myself in the wonder of a natural area and watch the show. I find it remarkable that one can observe a great blue heron land and take off while freeway traffic and airplanes buzz softly in the background.

Yankee Hill South

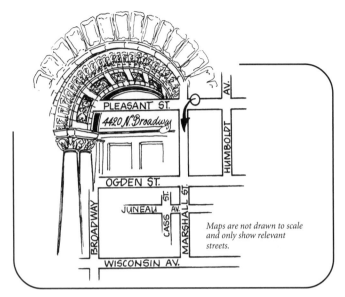

Maps are not drawn to scale and only show relevant streets.

Distance - 3 miles

HIGHLIGHTS
Many historic buildings, both private homes and commercial establishments

WHERE TO PARK
Close to 1012 East Pleasant Street

HOW TO GET THERE
Interstate 43 to North Avenue. East on North to Humboldt Avenue, south on Humboldt to Pleasant Street, west on Pleasant to 1012, a private home.

THE ROUTE
West on Pleasant to Marshall Street, south on Marshall to Wisconsin Avenue. West on Wisconsin to Broadway, north on Broadway to Ogden Street, east on Ogden to Marshall and back to start.

*Y*ankee Hill, with its well-placed home sites, was the center for turn-of-the-century luxurious comfort and Milwaukee's high society. I quote from *Milwaukee: At the Gathering of the Waters* by H. Anderson and F. Olson. "Indeed it is not easy to recall a quarter of any busy street which combines more comfort, evidences of wealth and taste and refinement, and a certain domestic character, than this portion of town on the bluffs, Prospect Avenue and the adjacent streets."

Yankee Hill, part of Juneautown, one of Milwaukee's three original settlements, is certainly the richest and most prestigious of those early neighborhoods. Solomon Juneau's original 160-acre claim, purchased for $1.25 an acre, was bordered by the Milwaukee River, Lake Michigan, East Wisconsin Avenue and Juneau Avenue. Juneau got the best part of the deal as Byron Kilbourn's 160 acres across the river were predominantly tamarack swamp and George Walker's section was a marsh with fingers of higher land jutting into it.

The walk begins four blocks north of Juneau Avenue and includes many of Milwaukee's important early residences and commercial buildings. As you walk, try to imagine those early settlers sitting high in elegant horse-drawn carriages in this wealthy neighborhood.

In 1901 Herman W. Buemming built his home at 1012 East Pleasant Street. It resembles a Greek temple with formal pillars and symmetrical design.

As you walk south on Marshall, notice St. Paul's Episcopal Church at Knapp Street. Built in 1883-84, it has beautiful stained glass windows created by the well-known Tiffany Studios in New York. A block farther south at Juneau Street, All Saint's Episcopal Cathedral has a cream city brick exterior trimmed with limestone and molded brick.

To see homes built in 1854 and 1874, detour one block west on Juneau to Cass Street. At 1219 North Cass, the William Metcalf residence is another cream city brick mansion trimmed with red sandstone quoins. At 1135 North Cass, the John

Dietrich Inbusch home is a square Italianate building with an exceptionally large 3½ foot cornice pierced by attic windows and supported by carved brackets.

Back on Marshall, watch for three elegant homes. The first, at 1119, built by wealthy ship owner Robert Patrick Fitzgerald, has a wooden cornice, an overhanging roof and paired brackets that support the overhang. Another Italianate home at 1029 has been remodeled seven times since it was built in 1855. If you look closely you can see the different window styles that illustrate the many changes made after this home's modest beginning.

A large impressive home at 817-819 Marshall was built as a double house in 1898 by two Baumgartens, Francis and Otto. Note the carved balustrade in front of the dormers and the molding where the walls meet the foundation.

When you get to Mason Street turn briefly west and walk through the Northwestern Mutual Life Insurance Park. The building, facing Wisconsin Avenue, was built in 1912. The impressive facade with ten Corinthian columns looks appropriate for a successful insurance company. Notice a touch of whimsy, horned gargoyles on the light fixtures.

Next you'll come to the Wisconsin Gas Company at 626. Built in 1929-30, it illustrates the then-progressive rectilinear skyscraper style of architecture.

Down the block and across the street at 517, the Federal Building is an excellent example of Romanesque architecture. Take a look inside to see the restoration, done in three phases to create a historically accurate interior.

The Milwaukee Club, built in 1883, is at the corner of Wisconsin and Jefferson Streets. This men's club still occupies the building. Across the street the Pfister Hotel has kept much of its original Victorian elegance, including a richly ornamented lobby.

When you come to Broadway turn north. Notice that this part of the walk showcases the juxtaposition of old and new in Milwaukee. Fortunately, city planners with foresight preserved many of Milwaukee's landmark buildings. Stand at the corner of Broadway and Wells, look north toward St. Mary's Catholic Church and east to the Plaza East Office Center to see fine examples of both 19th-century and late-20th-century architecture.

St. Mary's was Milwaukee's first German Roman Catholic church. Built in 1846, the year Milwaukee became a city, it houses a painting of the Annunciation, a gift from King Ludwig I of Bavaria.

Two blocks north at 1020 Broadway, the German-English Academy was built in 1890-91. It's decorated with terra cotta, and a scallop shell cornice. Walk one block farther north to see the Val Blatz Brewing Company Office Building at 1120 Broadway. Notice the limestone facade trimmed with sandstone and rusticated stone block carvings around the entrance, the windows and the pillars.

One block north and across the street at 1209 is Grace Lutheran Church. Built in 1900, it has three Gothic arches with sculptural spandrels over the entrance.

As you stand here and look west toward the colorful restored buildings on Water Street, it's evident something was lost when the freeway was built. Leave Broadway at Ogden Street and walk east back to Marshall and travel north on Marshall to Pleasant and back to start.

If you're hungry when you pass Eddie Glorioso's Italian Market, you can buy fixings for a sandwich from the deli or have them make a twelve inch sub sandwich for a picnic.

There's more to see on this walk than the buildings I described. Take some time to explore these side streets and you'll be amazed as I am by the restoration and renewal taking place on Milwaukee's Lower East Side.

The Final Exam - Layton Boulevard

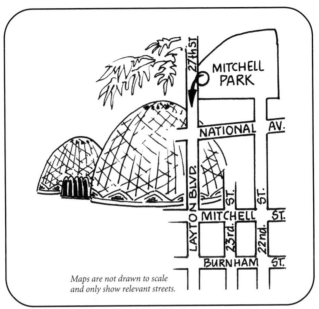

Maps are not drawn to scale and only show relevant streets.

Distance - 3 miles

HIGHLIGHTS

   Turn-of-the-century homes on Layton Boulevard, Frank Lloyd Wright homes, Mitchell Park

WHERE TO PARK

   In the parking lot in Mitchell Park close to the Domes

HOW TO GET THERE

   Interstate 94 west to 27th Street exit. Follow 27th south across the bridge to Mitchell Park.

THE ROUTE

   Leave Mitchell Park and walk south on Layton Boulevard to Burnham Street. East on Burnham to 23rd, north on 23rd to Mitchell, east on Mitchell Street to 22nd Street, north on 22nd back to Mitchell Park. Go north and west in the park back to start.

This walk starts and ends in Mitchell Park, a must-see stop for out-of-town guests. Since 1964 the three domes, desert, tropical and temperate have been showplaces for massive cacti, delicate tropical orchids and lavish seasonal displays. The domes, each 87 feet high and 140 feet across, replaced a plant conservatory that had been built in 1898 and completed in 1904 with the addition of sunken gardens. Most people who come to Mitchell Park come to see the domes, but the rest of the park is nice too. It's one of Milwaukee's earliest public parks.

Leave the park and turn south on Layton Boulevard. At 1434, take a look at St. Lawrence Catholic Church, a Romanesque design built in 1905. Next at 1501 you'll come to St. Joseph's Convent Chapel, another Romanesque Revival church built in 1914 for the Sisters of St. Francis. At 1545 you'll see Sacred Heart Sanitarium with its five story brick tower. It was originally built for hydrotherapy and had a spa-like atmosphere. Later it became the first hospital in Wisconsin to be devoted to physical rehabilitation. Today it's called the Sacred Heart Rehabilitation Hospital.

In the next block at 1615, a home designed to resemble a rustic German cottage was built in 1923 by Dr. Urban A. Schlueter. Inspired by idealized storybook illustrations of cozy domestic charm, it has a picture postcard ambiance. The architect, Walter Truettner, called himself "the bungalow man," because he specialized in unique bungalows reminiscent of European cottages.

As you ramble down Layton Boulevard, try to imagine it as the Indian trail that ran from Chicago to Green Bay. By the mid-1800s this trail was surrounded by early settlers' farms and adjacent farmland. By the 1880s this bucolic farmland began to be divided into country estates. Later, Mitchell Park was developed, streetcar lines were laid and a car barn was built at 27th and National. Residents from Walker's Point to the east moved to this area to build new homes. By the early 1900s, Layton Boulevard was the center of South Side society.

Just for fun, between National Avenue and Burnham Street, see how many architectural features you can identify on the homes, built by prominent South Side residents one hundred years ago. Here are a few I found as I walked these several blocks:

colonnades   cornices   block modillions
quatrefoils   tympana   dentils
lintels   quoins   brackets
pediments   friezes   gable roof lines
eyebrow windows   conical roofs

As you locate these fourteen features, it's acceptable to write in the book! Some readers may know more about this than I do but for the uninitiated, this should prove to be an interesting, if not frustrating challenge. What's important is the ability to look. The more you look, the more you will see!

As you walk farther south, the homes get smaller. Notice the bungalows between Mitchell and Maple Streets with similar, yet different design features. When you come to Burnham, detour one block west to see the Frank Lloyd Wright homes. One of Wright's goals was to build affordable homes for middle-income families. The four duplexes and two single-family homes designed by Wright are built of pre-cut lumber according to standardized designs. Since they're built on small lots, their inside dimensions are modest, yet these homes have the clean lines and ageless appeal typical of Wright's work.

Walk east on Burnham, north on 23rd to Mitchell Street, east on Mitchell to 22nd Street and north on 22nd back to the park. You'll see many dilapidated Polish flats and bungalows, some in better condition than others. One can see how this neighborhood has changed from a working class area where everyone knew their neighbors and Polish pride in home ownership was a way of life, to an area on the skids. Once homes cease to be owner-occupied, urban rot often sets in.

When you get to the park, follow the path to the left past

the pond. Here people fish for trout as part of Milwaukee's Urban Fishing Program. On a balmy August day when I came by, old men, teenagers and young families all had lines in the water hoping to catch a stocked trout. The limit is three but I don't think that's a problem for these ever-hopeful fisherpeople.

From here you can return to start or take a detour to the northeast corner of the park. There you'll step back in time to 1795 and the site where Jacque Vieau built his cabin, the first home built in Milwaukee. Vieau established a Northwest Fur Company trading site at this location because it was close to both the Green Bay-Chicago Trail and the Menomonee River.

After touring Milwaukee's neighborhoods, north, south, east, west, city, suburb, some grand homes and some not, it's appropriate to end this walking guide at the site of Milwaukee's first home. I hope you enjoyed the journey!

Layton Boulevard

When Frederick Layton died in 1919, the "Milwaukee Sentinel" proclaimed, "Milwaukee has lost its best loved, most honored citizen." In 1888 Layton had given the city its first art museum, and he continued to furnish it with European works of art the rest of his life. Layton was a philanthropist to such an extent that by the time he died at the age of 93 he had given away most of his wealth.

When this boulevard was named by ordinance in 1909, it was the only street in the city to bear Layton's name. A second was added later as Milwaukee expanded southward and Layton Avenue became part of the city.

Bibliography

Ethnic Buildings, The Milwaukee Department of City Development.

Ethnic Homes, The Milwaukee Department of City Development.

The Greendale Historical Society Tour Guide, Greendale Historical Society.

The Heritage Guidebook, H. Russell Zimmermann, Harry W. Schwartz, 1989.

Milwaukee: At the Gathering of the Waters, Harry H. Anderson and Frederick I. Olson, Continental Heritage Press, 1981.

Milwaukee Streets: The Stories Behind Their Names, Carl Baehr, Cream City Press, 1995.

Outdoor Sculpture in Milwaukee, Diane Buck and Virginia Palmer, State Historical Society of Wisconsin, 1995.